Boston Fire
in the Church

How to Prevent and Extinguish Fires of
Negativity Within Your Church

Brandon Lewis

Boston Fire in the Church: How to Prevent and Extinguish Fires of Negativity Within Your church

ISBN: 978-1-7934-4815-6 (Usable only with Kindle Direct Publishing)

Published by Brandon Lewis Publishing
Spartanburg, SC

For permission, contact: BostonFireInTheChurch@gmail.com

Scripture quotations are from The ESV® Bible (The Holy Bible, English Standard Version®), copyright © 2001 by Crossway, a publishing ministry of Good News Publishers. Used by permission. All rights reserved. Print edition: 2016.

To my beloved wife Amy and our amazing children:
Hannah, Micah, Caden, and Josiah.
I love you.

Contents

Acknowledgements

Thank you to Amy Lewis (my wife), Pastor Randy and Dr. Oley Lewis (my parents), and to Pastors Daniel Godfrey (Director of Missions of the Broad River Baptist Association) and Dr. Jim Goodroe (former Director of Missions of the Spartanburg County Baptist Network) for reading drafts of this book, offering advice, and encouraging me. You have been invaluable to me.

Thank you to Rick Harrison of The History Channel's *Pawn Stars*. Hearing you briefly talk about locked fire call boxes on your show many years ago is what set things in motion. Your remarks really intrigued me, I began investigating, and the rest is history!

Above all, thank you to my Heavenly Father for every "good and perfect gift" (James 1:17) that you made available to me as I was writing this book. Those gifts were many, but the guidance, strength, and encouragement that you continuously provided were especially appreciated. This is *your* book. May it bring you glory!

Preface:
The Purpose of this Book

You may be aware of the Great Chicago Fire that occurred in October of 1871. People still mention this fire on occasion, and some still toss around the humorous but long-debunked notion that the fire was started by a cow that kicked over a lantern. The Great Chicago Fire is an event that is widely known, and many history books ensure that it won't be easily forgotten.

Sadly, the same can't be said of the Great Boston Fire of 1872, which occurred just over a year after the Great Chicago Fire. Although it remains the largest and most destructive fire in Boston's history, as well as one of the costliest fires in American history, the Great Boston Fire never garnered the lasting respect and awe as did its predecessor in Chicago. Many history books fail to mention it, and even historical museums within the city of Boston fail to properly exhibit the epic fire that once brought so much devastation to one of America's most historic cities.

The common oversight of this event is unfortunate. The Great Boston Fire is a unique and incredibly intriguing story that offers so many profound insights, messages, and warnings to those willing to delve into the details of the event. In fact, examining some of those very details is one of the purposes of this book, and yet its primary focus regards something far greater than merely bringing to light commonly overlooked pieces of historical information. This book's utmost purpose and mission is to comparatively use information about the great fire in a discussion about figurative fires of negativity that occur within modern churches and how you and your church can go about effectively combating these fires. The hope behind this book is that God would allow a nearly forgotten fire that occurred so many years ago to be used to get your attention, to be paralleled with various principles within his Word, and to bring you to a better understanding of how to effectively prevent and extinguish the church-crippling fires of negativity that our arsonist-enemy Satan is hoping will destroy your church!

In the same way the city of Boston faced a literal and devastating fire in 1872, today's churches face figurative fires of division and discord that have the potential to destroy much (if not all) of what God has purposed various churches to be and do for his kingdom. These dangerous fires come in an array of forms, from gossip and bickering to demoralizing power wars, along with many things in between. God's people desperately need to be aware of how to prevent these fires from occurring and how to quickly extinguish others that nevertheless pop up on occasion. As you and others within your church read and absorb a host of lessons gleaned from Boston's tragedy that have been intertwined with biblical instruction, efforts and strategies can then be wisely employed to go about fireproofing and saving your church from destruction.

The learning will be interesting and challenging, but it will also be transforming and empowering for the life of your church. If you're determined to let God's Word dictate how you deal with fires of negativity, you can go ahead and say, "There will be no Boston fire in *my* church!" As you and others within your church begin applying the biblical principles identified within this book, you'll make sure of it. Let the fireproofing begin!

1

The Great Boston Fire of 1872
Your Church Could Face Its Own Boston Fire

A t approximately 7:20pm, on Saturday, November 9th, 1872, a four-story commercial warehouse in the heart of Boston's financial district began to burn. Located on the corner of the Southeastern intersection of Summer Street and Kingston Street in downtown Boston, the building had already been vacated by everyone who worked within it when the fire began to rage, as business hours had long ended. Within the building's basement was a small steam engine that powered the building's elevator, and it is believed that a random spark or an unnoticed coal that may have accidentally been raked out of the furnace hours earlier was responsible for ultimately setting the building ablaze. Regardless of how the fire started, it steadily and rapidly grew. The building was stocked with an abundance of dry goods that fueled the fire, and the building's elevator most likely acted as a flue that swiftly propelled the fire from one story of the building to the next.

After consuming the place of its origin, the fire went on to destroy an additional 775 buildings within Boston. The great fire raged for more than 12 hours and covered more than 60 acres before being completely extinguished by Boston's fire department, and thus it only took about half a day for several hundred businesses to be annihilated, thousands of Bostonians to be rendered jobless, and nearly 1000 Bostonians to lose their homes. Most tragically, the great fire required the lives of more than a dozen individuals (some reports suggest it could have been as high as 30), and all because Boston had been ill-prepared to prevent or extinguish a fire of this magnitude.

Repeated warnings of the city's all-too-perfect conditions for a fiery doom had gone unheeded by city officials. Boston's fire department had never been properly equipped to combat enormous fires, despite Fire Chief John Damrell's numerous attempts to acquire better equipment and to create and enforce fire codes. Like most Bostonians, city officials had foolishly believed that a monstrous fire would never happen in their city. They had mentally relegated fiery atrocities to other places, such as Chicago. The idea that had reigned-supreme in the hearts of most Bostonians, regarding the potential for an overwhelmingly destructive fire, was one of immunity: "Certainly not here. Somewhere else, maybe. But not here." And yet, a great fire *did* happen in Boston, and it remains the most tragic fire Boston has ever faced. As you'll come to learn in the following chapters, Bostonians had no one to blame for their city's enormous loss but themselves.

Satan Wants a Boston Fire to Destroy Your Church

Satan would like nothing more than to convince you and others in your church that your particular "fellowship of believers" is special and immune to destructive fires that figuratively burn churches to the ground. He wants you and others to believe that egregious church fires only happen elsewhere. And yet, this kind of foolish thinking (if adopted) will prevent you and your church from taking necessary measures to prevent and extinguish church fires, and then Satan will do whatever it takes to start a heinous fire right under your noses and watch it inevitably damage or destroy the work that God is doing in your church.

Satan loves to throw fiery darts wherever he thinks those darts will land with the most ferocity, and a church that is unsuspecting and unaware of how to faithfully "extinguish the flaming darts of the evil one" (Ephesians 6:16) can easily fall prey to a figurative Boston fire. For instance, negativity may raise its ugly head in the form of arguments and disagreements that pop up within the church, or maybe it will be a sin among church leadership that gets purposefully overlooked or mishandled. Negativity might come in the form of one or more church members who choose to sow gossip and discord, or it may come when an outsider with nefarious intentions infiltrates your church and tries to corral a following. Indeed, there is no shortage of fiery darts of negativity in Satan's arsenal (as only a few examples have been listed here), and he'll try to use any or all of them to produce a Boston fire of sorts within your church, if he thinks he can get away with it!

3

A church that believes it is somehow innately protected from negativity and its consequences is a church much like Boston's city officials had been before the great fire. It's a church that refuses to see reality for what it is. It's a church that chooses to believe that everything will be fine all by itself. These are the churches that ultimately face growing fires of negativity that go on to produce a collective pain across the membership, and sometimes these fires can produce a mass exodus of members, a church split, or a church fold. In the least, these fires can cause churches that may not suffer a declining membership to nevertheless struggle at remaining effective at pursuing their God-ordained missions.

For Satan to be defeated, regarding his efforts to destroy churches with raging fires of negativity, churches must become skilled at preventing fires and extinguishing fires before it's too late. A mentality of apathy and false security must be tossed aside, and purposeful and strategic action must be employed. While the following chapters will guide you through tried and true biblical strategies that you can use to fireproof your church, you should first make an important decision before reading them. Decide *now* if you're going to take seriously the devastating threat that hangs over your church or if you're content with hoping (or pretending) that a divine forcefield of sorts is always going to keep your church free from Boston fires, without any effort on your part.

If you're having trouble making your decision, consider why the Apostle Paul stressed that all believers should gear up in figurative battle armor to fight Satan and extinguish his flaming darts (Ephesians 6:10-18). It's simply because there are no divine forcefields. God expects each of us to follow the direction of his Word to defeat Satan, and we must do that collectively as fellow believers to thwart Satan from burning down our churches with negativity.

The Lady and the Mirror

Maybe your church is already long-entrenched within a monstrous fire of division and discord, and you believe severe and irreparable damage has already occurred within your church. Despite the pain that you and others are feeling, and despite the devastating fires that may still linger and threaten your church even further, perhaps you've chosen to passionately and fearfully hold on to any small vestige of your church that has yet to be annihilated, such as a few remaining friendships, an involvement in a small group, or an aspect of a ministry in which you're serving. Maybe you're holding on with dear life, as you hope that somehow the destruction that has already occurred elsewhere in your church won't make its way to one or two of the last remaining pieces of your church that you still believe to be good and worth protecting for as long as possible – that is, unless and until complete destruction takes place and the church ceases to exist.

Perhaps your plight is like that of a woman who was witnessed hastily carrying a large vanity mirror down Devonshire Street when the great fire was having its way with Boston. Although the mirror was cracked in many directions and large pieces of it had fallen out, the woman kept a tight grasp on the mirror as she rushed through the crowd of onlookers. Every now and then, the woman would look over her shoulder in the direction of the fire, and her eyes would fill with fear. After one such look, the woman decided to begin running as quickly as she could. Not long afterward, she tripped and fell onto the pavement, and the mirror she had been carrying completely disintegrated underneath her; pieces of the mirror were scattered all around her. Without delay, the woman picked herself up and gathered as many pieces of the mirror as she could gather. Holding the broken fragments of the mirror to her heart, the woman proceeded to frantically make her way down the road.

Maybe you're traveling down a road of despair as you figuratively hold broken pieces of your hurting and fragmented church closely to your heart. Perhaps you're hoping against all odds that somehow, by some miracle, those pieces can be salvaged and restored and that your church can rise from beneath the ashes of negativity and exist once again for God's glory. While the woman with the mirror certainly never saw her mirror in working order again (at least not pertaining to those particular broken fragments of the mirror that she was carrying around), the same doesn't have to be true of your church and the many wonderful pieces of it that were once used by God in incredible ways. As awful as the damage of fires may be in your church, it's *possible* that God may choose to restore your church and allow its many pieces to once again be united in reflecting his message to a community that so desperately needs him. Conversely, it's also possible that God will choose to allow your church to come to a permanent end, while he ultimately begins or continues reaching your community through other churches and ministries.

One thing is certain: if your church is going to make a comeback, God will be the one who ordains this to happen, and he'll use you and others in your church to carry out rebuilding efforts. From the start, those efforts will consist of many fire extinguishing and fireproofing measures that are presented within the following chapters of this book. You can learn these strategies and begin employing them in your current fellowship even now, as you and others begin or continue to vigorously pray about God's direction and purpose for your church. Indeed, God may decide to give your church new life. This is the hope! He *has* been known to do this, mind you.

The worst-case scenario entails your being able to help fireproof a new body of believers to which God sends you if your current church isn't on track for a divine rebound. If God directs you to another church, you don't need to take with you any of the negativity or lack of skills, regarding extinguishing and preventing fires, that may have contributed to your previous church's demise. Instead, you can become an immediate asset to your new church, as you faithfully employ fire extinguishing and fireproofing techniques that you learn within this book. Therefore, prepare to dig-in and learn all you can, because this knowledge is going to be crucial for you and your church, regardless of whether it's the church you're in now or the one to which God will direct you down the line.

We're All Called to Be Firefighters

The Great Boston Fire brought widespread destruction and pain to a city that had numerous firefighters. Those firefighters were trained well, and most of them vehemently endeavored to keep their city safe from fires. Each of them no doubt abhorred the idea of their city being destroyed by a fire, so they probably did everything within their power to prevent fires and extinguish others. But on one particular Saturday, their efforts were not enough. Boston's firefighters were outmatched by a fire that would ultimately go down in history for springing up and catching a city off guard and ill-prepared.

The outcome would have been altogether different had the city of Boston been comprised of citizens (each and every one) who were at least somewhat interested and involved in preventing and extinguishing fires. If every single Bostonian had felt a responsibility to protect the city from fires and to learn and employ methods and procedures to safeguard the city, Boston's trained firefighters would have had the help they needed to severely minimize the fire's effect on the city. Mind you, not every citizen would have had to become an official firefighter serving within the fire department, but every citizen could have taken personal steps toward fire prevention, thus making Boston a safer place.

The same is true of our churches. Well trained pastors, staff, and other leaders cannot rightly be expected to thwart and extinguish every church fire all by themselves. Each church must be comprised of members (ideally, each and every one) who are supremely interested and involved in preventing and extinguishing fires. Not everyone is called and equipped to serve as a pastor or within any number of other positions, but each church member can and should become skilled at helping to keep satanic fires from destroying God's purpose within a church.

Church members are called to consistently "meet together", to "encourage one another", and to "stir up one another to love and good works" (Hebrews 10:24-25). Faithfully fending-off fires of negativity is a significant part of stirring up and promoting a continuation of love and good works within a church body. A church cannot love and serve at a maximum level while fires are allowed to rage and threaten the church's very existence. The author of Hebrews said it this way: "Let *us* consider how to stir up one another." Therefore, the stirring and the firefighting are responsibilities that belong to each one of *us*. No one can rightly blame any one individual or group of people (from pastors to lay members) for a destructive church fire that damages a church. Fighting fires is a collective effort. Therefore, each and every church member should be a firefighter in one way or another, ready and willing to do his part to safeguard his church.

If you're ready to help fireproof your church, your training will begin in the next chapter. Read and prayerfully apply what you learn, and then pray for others within your church family who may be reading this book along with you. Ask God to help every willing individual within your church to become proficient and active at collectively preventing and extinguishing destructive fires. And then don't drop the ball! Always do *your* part within that collective effort, even when it's difficult. Your church is counting on you!

2

Fire Call Boxes Were Locked
Never Lock Up Your Ministry Potential

Boston was one of the first cities in the United States to strategically place fire call boxes around the city. These call boxes were metal units that sat atop a concrete structure that made them about eye level for most adults. When these call boxes were used properly, a citizen wishing to quickly report a fire to the city's fire department would simply open a door on the box and proceed to turn a little crank a certain number of times, as per instructions posted within the box. This would then produce a telling ring at various fire stations that would notify firemen of the most approximate location of the fire, as each call box sent out its own recognizable ring. Stations nearest the triggered call box would then be among the first to quickly deploy firemen to the scene.

Unfortunately, however, city officials had decided to lock up all call boxes several years before the great fire had occurred. The decision was made because quite a few children and adults had allowed their mischievous spirits to get the best of them in previous years, as they purposefully used the call boxes to sound false alarms.

Because of these pranks, city officials had decided that locking the call boxes was the only way to thwart unwarranted alarms going forward, even though doing so would almost completely nullify the efficacy of the call boxes altogether. Therefore, to prevent erroneous alarms from being made while simultaneously hoping to keep the call boxes at least somewhat useful, city officials decided to grant call box access to select individuals, such as bank presidents, market owners, and police officers. These individuals were called "upstanding citizens", according to the consensus of city officials, and they were thus deemed worthy to be given special keys that would unlock the call boxes.

Sadly, there were no city-ordained "upstanding citizens" around when the great fire began as a humble fire in the basement of a warehouse near call box number 52. Rather, a handful of teenage boys who were playing in the streets had been the first to notice the fire, as the windows of the warehouse had signaled them with a telling glow. Upon observation, the boys ran to the nearest call box (52) to trigger the alarm, only to learn that it had been locked. Realizing they couldn't trigger the alarm, the boys began screaming at the top of their lungs about the fire as they ran through the streets. They were hoping someone would hear their cries and come to the rescue. As for tracking down a shop owner or someone else who had been given a key to the call box (if the boys had even been aware of the protocol), they would have had no luck, as most of these "upstanding citizens" had already closed their businesses for the day and had vacated the area.

Ultimately, about 20 minutes after the fire had first

been spotted by the teenagers, a police officer with a call box key happened upon the area and noticed the burning warehouse and the teenage boys running and yelling in the streets. Soon afterward, the officer unlocked the call box and sounded the first alarm. In the moments that followed, he sounded a second alarm. Unfortunately, by the time firemen had been made aware of the fire, it had already grown to monstrous proportions.

City officials who studied the fire and interviewed eyewitnesses in the days and weeks after the fire was extinguished agreed that the fire would have been far less devastating had the alarm from call box number 52 been triggered when the fire had first been noticed by the teenage boys. Furthermore, fire experts later estimated that those 20 minutes of delay could have made all the difference in the world, regarding the fire department's ability to have contained the fire before it had spread beyond a few buildings.

Perhaps if Boston's call boxes had never been locked at all, the greater part of the city's financial district wouldn't have burned down. Of course, this would have meant the city would have had to continue dealing with call box misuse and abuse, as annoying false alarms would have inevitably continued to be an issue, but it would have probably been well worth it overall. Instead, without the possibility of being used inappropriately, locked call boxes stood throughout the city of Boston merely looking good, giving people a sense of false security, having great potential to be tools used to spare lives and property (if not for being locked), but being almost entirely worthless – save the rare occasion wherein an "upstanding citizen" might happen to be at the right place at the right time.

Locked Fire Call Boxes Exist Within the Church

Figuratively speaking, locked call boxes exist within many of God's churches today. They're Christ followers who have great potential to be tools used in God's kingdom, but because these individuals have been misused, abused, and unappreciated by others in the past, they have locked up their ministerial potential by refusing to use the gifts that God has given them to serve others in the family of God. Their motto could very well be stated like the old idiom, "once bitten, twice shy," for they care more about ensuring that they're never hurt again than they do about their God-given abilities being used for God's purposes.

These figurative call boxes are individuals who try to justify their refusals to serve God and others by saying things to themselves (and sometimes even to others) that sound like this:

> - "I'll never be hurt again. I'm going to continue going to church (some don't even do that), but no one better expect me to do a thing."

> - "No one will ever take advantage of me again. Who do people think they are – that they can run over me, embarrass me, and trample all over my feelings? I'm not a floor mat! This won't ever happen again; my days of serving are finished."

- "I'll not serve where I'm not appreciated. If people aren't willing to recognize and respect my God-given abilities, then I'll shut down my services altogether."

Equipped with hurting and defensive attitudes, these never-abuse-me-again call boxes often attend churches while merely *pretending* they're invested in their church, as they remain unwilling to faithfully "serve one another" with their gifts (1 Peter 4:10). And thus, similar to the locked call boxes of Boston, these individuals may look good in the church (in as much as they help fill the seats), but they're unknowingly contributing to a false sense of security among others within the church who may be unaware that these individuals are determined to hold out when it comes to their being on the giving (serving) end of ministry, while their proclivity is to remain solely on the receiving end.

The Fiery Repercussions of Locked Fire Call Boxes Within the Church

When Christ followers refuse to use their abilities to minister within their churches, many negative church fires can start or grow. For instance, undue stresses on those who *are* serving within the church begin to mount, as they struggle to minister effectively while ministry needs often become more than they can bear. This is due in part because of locked call boxes who refuse to step up and serve. In fact, in many churches, about 80 percent of the ministry that occurs is performed by only about 20 percent of the people within the church family, as the old adage goes. This means that merely a few individuals are carrying all the weight of ministry, and they have no other option but to naturally drop the ball in a multitude of ways, no matter how strong their faith in Christ may be. Moreover, these servants are no doubt missing opportunities to reach and disciple various individuals, as they're overworked and focused on too many things. As a result, many come to experience ministerial burnout, which renders these individuals broken and ill-equipped to continue ministering. Sadly, some of these individuals ultimately decide that they must remove themselves from ministry entirely, as they become locked call boxes of their own. This series of events makes an already-desperate situation even worse, like winds that propel an existing fire to grow and burn even more uncontrollably.

Sometimes senior pastors, elders, or other staff members are the ones who decide to clam up and leave the ministry altogether after suffering incredible hurt within the church, and their often premature and abrupt departures sometimes allow a church fire to start or grow to such a degree as to annihilate the shepherd-less or undersupplied church body that they leave behind. A handful of studies reveal that hundreds of pastors within the United States permanently leave the ministry each month. It should therefore be no surprise that thousands of churches close their doors each year; some of these churches have no pastoral leadership and cannot acquire such in a timely manner.

Simply stated, locked call boxes wreak havoc on a church, and churches that can nevertheless survive the problems of locked call boxes without being totally devastated still suffer tremendously. No church remains completely unscathed when members (either laity or leadership) decide to become locked call boxes.

Satan's "Upstanding Citizen" Ploy

Satan absolutely loves to start and feed nasty church fires by convincing people to withhold their God-given talents and abilities from service. While it otherwise might be a very difficult task for him to convince many Christ followers to abandon their services, as many who have been hurt continue to have a passion for serving and understand its importance, Satan will dangle the "upstanding citizen" ploy as an enticement when he needs to do so. In other words, Satan will try to convince individuals that there will come a time and a place wherein they'll finally be able to minister without ever facing the possibility of being hurt again. Satan tells individuals that there will be "upstanding citizens" (perfect individuals, groups, and churches) who will *unlock* opportunities for them to engage within pain-free ministry without ever suffering any misuse and abuse. When Christ followers take the bait, they shut down their services and decide to wait on their "upstanding citizen" moment to come around – but it never happens. In reality, there are no completely pain-free ministry opportunities, just as there are no perfect individuals, groups, and churches. Within every ministry, there will always be a degree of misuse and abuse that exists among sinful individuals, including Christ followers.

Jesus Had Plenty of Reasons to Be a Locked Fire Call Box

If anyone ever had an abundance of reasons to shut down and refuse to minister, it was Jesus. Many people hurt him, took advantage of him, and under-appreciated him, but he never threw in the towel; he continued to minister. Ill-treatment from others never deterred him from doing exactly what God had appointed him to do.

For instance, on one occasion, religious leaders charged Jesus with being demonic, and they tried to stone him to death (John 8:48-9:7). Jesus literally had to hide himself in order to slip away from his would-be murderers. Immediately afterward, Jesus was not seen flustered, calling it quits, or lamenting about the outrageous abuse he had just suffered; he was seen healing a man who had been born blind.

On another occasion, Jesus' own family tried to hinder him from his ministry (Mark 3:20-35). They demanded that Jesus stop what he was doing, regarding preaching to a large crowd without taking time to eat, and they tried to highjack his meeting. Nevertheless, Jesus continued to minister. He did not throw up his hands in surrender and say, "Well, if my own family doesn't appreciate what I'm doing, I might as well just forget about ministry altogether!"

Jesus' own disciples often treated him no better than did his biological family and the religious leaders of his day. Peter rebuked him and later denied knowing him (Matthew 16:22 and John 18:19-27), Judas turned against him and betrayed him (Luke 22:48), and not one of his disciples gave Jesus the support he needed during one of his most trying of circumstances, when he was agonizingly pouring out his soul to God in the hours before his crucifixion (Luke 22:39-46). And yet, Jesus did not stop doing what he was appointed to do even then. He persisted with his mission.

Even after Jesus had been arrested, beaten, humiliated, mocked, and hung on a cross to die, Jesus refused to cease and desist when it came to ministry. While on the cross, Jesus said several things that ministered to onlookers and others who were near him. He also ministered to his own mother (John 19:26-27) and to a thief hanging on the cross beside him (Luke 23:43). Up until Jesus took his final breath, he continued to minister to others.

Absolutely *nothing* convinced Jesus to become a locked call box; he continued to minister in *all* circumstances, even when others were hurting him, taking advantage of him, and under-appreciating him. We should follow his example. There are too many fires that rage within our churches to do anything else. Every Christ follower should always be ministering in some capacity, and ill-treatment from others should never persuade us to do otherwise. May we never forget that our gifts and talents belong to God, and we therefore have no right to lock them up or bury them (Matthew 25:25) just because we face trying and uncomfortable circumstances. As our example, Jesus took the form of a servant and humbled himself to the point of death on a cross, and we are called to minister unto others with that same mindset as our constant motivation

(Philippians 2:5-8). Therefore, Christ followers should always be engaged in serving others, even in the face of abuse.

Ministry Stinks Sometimes, But We do it Anyway

In a perfect world, Christ followers would never face abuse while ministering unto others. There would never be individuals who need to be counseled or disciplined by others within the church for their abusive actions, and nobody would ever feel led by the Holy Spirit to take their God-given talents someplace else (albeit, to another imperfect place, perhaps merely better suited to receive them) because their current situation consists of those who refuse to grow in Christ and respond appropriately to their ministry. But since a perfect world does not exist, these steps must be taken from time to time, and they each can be an appropriate response to abuse when done biblically.

What's *not* a biblically-ordained response is when Christ followers permanently stop serving the body of Christ altogether when they have suffered abuse. (However, temporary sabbaticals for healing and recovery, when necessary, are a different story. Here, we are talking about would-be *permanent* ministry shutdowns based on bitter, defensive, sometimes vindictive, and largely selfish attitudes of those who have suffered within ministry and want to ensure it never happens again). Locked call boxes have no appropriate place within any church. We are each called to serve one another faithfully, no matter how pleasant or unpleasant our circumstances may be.

The fact is simply this: ministry stinks sometimes. Abuse happens, and yet, we should continue to minister and watch the power of God move mightily in people's lives. Each of us should have "a lamb's heart and a lizard's skin" (as the late Dr. Jim Akins used to say) when it comes to ministering to others, meaning we should always gently and lovingly minister and interact with others while not allowing ourselves to be too sensitive to the abuses that come our way in the process.

The Apostle Paul would second that admonition, for he explained the awesome end-results that occur when we continue to minister through rough times and abuse: "We are afflicted in every way, but not crushed; perplexed, but not driven to despair; persecuted, but not forsaken; struck down, but not destroyed; always carrying in the body the death of Jesus, so that the life of Jesus may also be manifested in our bodies. For we who live are always being given over to death for Jesus' sake, so that the life of Jesus also may be manifested in our mortal flesh. So death is at work in us, but life in you" (2 Corinthians 4:8-12).

Did you catch that? While *death* is at work within those of us who minister, *life* is at work within those to whom we minister. In other words, Paul was saying, "Sometimes it feels like we are physically losing everything (even our own lives) while we minister within rough circumstances, but the pay-off comes in how that ministry affects others, by way of birthing and growing spiritual life!" It's an easy decision when you think of

21

ministry with the appropriate mindset. Ministry makes new life possible, while locked call boxes do not.

If you would like to see your church preventing and extinguishing destructive fires, then do your part. Choose never to be a locked call box! Just as each call box in Boston had a distinctive ring of its own, you do as well! You are the only person who can minister in the very specific way that God has enabled you to minister, so always be of service in his kingdom. Take the appropriate steps to unlock yourself unto ministry if you aren't already serving. When abuse comes your way, simply roll with the punches, while thanking God for using you to minister unto others. When your ego begins to bruise and your selfish tendencies try to convince you that you are too valuable to be mistreated by others, remind yourself of Christ and his example, and then press on. Your church will be better, safer, and stronger for it!

3

Gas Supply Lines Were Not Shut Off
Know When and How to Bless Others

In 1872, it was gas rather than electricity that fueled businesses and homes. Gas was a wonderful thing; it provided light, warmth, and a means whereby food could be cooked. Regarding outdoor lighting, gas street lamps were everywhere. Boston was a big and beautiful city, and people could observe its majesty at all hours of the day, thanks to the gas supply lines that ran under the city's buildings and streets.

However, after the onset of the fire, Boston's gas supply lines soon went from being a blessing to being a curse. The same gas lines that provided power for so many great and needed things prior to the fire became supply lines of fuel *for* the fire. It was a nightmare; gas explosions rocked the city in numerous areas, and these explosions greatly fed pre-existing fires and even started many new ones.

For the longest time, city officials chose not to shut off the gas supply lines. There were concerns, regarding unlit streets and neighborhoods making looting more undetectable, that prevented officials from shutting off the gas in the earlier stages of the fire. In fact, it was not until several days after the fire began that officials ultimately decided to turn off the city's gas, in part because they grew tired of the continued explosions and the new fires being set ablaze by the uncontrolled gas lines. Ultimately, had Boston's gas lines been shut off at the onset of the original fire, it would have gone a long way in aiding the city's efforts to extinguish the fire, and it would have prevented other fires from occurring.

When Blessings are Curses Within the Church

Just like Boston's gas supply lines, each of us have the potential to be a tremendous blessing to others on regular occasion. As Christ followers, we are called to consistently bless others in a variety of ways simply because we are brothers and sisters within Christ's family. For example, we are to encourage our brothers and sisters in Christ by rejoicing with them in happy times and mourning with them in times of sadness (Romans 12:15). We are to restore our brothers and sisters in Christ when they have been caught in sin (Galatians 6:1). We are to provide for our brothers and sisters when they're in financial need (Acts 4:34-35, Ephesians 4:28). And this list goes on!

When we set out to bless others in ways that God's Word has prescribed, we have the potential to be a tremendous blessing. However, just like Boston's gas supply lines, we can become a curse to others by saying and doing things in the wrong time and in the wrong way – even when our intentions are pure. One proverb speaks directly to this: "Whoever blesses his neighbor with a loud voice, rising early in the morning, will be counted as cursing" (Proverbs 27:14).

You might have thought that blessing a neighbor would *always* be a very positive thing, but when a blessing is carried out at the wrong time (for instance, too early in the morning) and in the wrong way (for instance, with a loud voice), a curse can be the result. What would otherwise be a very positive thing can indeed become a curse simply because of the manner and timing of the blessing's bestowal.

Sadly, there are times all of us within the church get the timing and the manner wrong when it comes to our attempts to bless others. You can probably think of several episodes in your past wherein you thought you were doing something great for someone or a group of people, and your words or actions backfired and royally offended the very ones to whom you were trying to minister. It's like we are gas supply lines that are fueling blessings unto others in one moment, and then we're fueling hurt and negativity at other moments – all while trying to solely do the former. Sometimes, it seems like we don't know exactly how or when to say the right thing or do the right thing, and so we haphazardly guess our way through it all while merely hoping our efforts will make matters better instead of worse.

We must understand that our best efforts to bless others can make matters worse when not done in the right time and in the right way. Even our efforts to stop fiery situations within our churches can be done with the best of intentions and still backfire on us and make matters worse. Because of this, we must know *when* and *how* to bless others before going forward; therefore, the timing and the manner of our efforts must be directed by God.

When We Seek Him, He Will Guide Us

When we need to know exactly when and how to say and do the right things, to bring about blessings instead of curses (and to help extinguish church fires instead of fuel them), we can allow God's Holy Spirit within us to instruct us. When we seek God's direction, he will never leave us in the dark; he will speak to us through his Word and through his voice. His Word repeatedly makes this clear! For example, Jesus said that those who take the initiative to inquire of God will receive the answers that they need (Matthew 7:7-11). He encouraged us to be askers and seekers, and he promised us that our Heavenly Father wouldn't disappoint us by failing to respond.

Additionally, the biblical author of James wrote of asking God for wisdom. Divine wisdom is very needed for anyone desiring to know when and how to go about blessing others. James wrote, "If any of you lacks wisdom, let him ask God, who gives generously to all without reproach, and it will be given to him" (James 1:5). The part about him giving generously "without reproach" means that God won't shame you or rebuke you for your upfront approach in asking him outright for wisdom. Instead, he will honor your request and give you exactly what you need. Providing you with needed wisdom delights God, which is why he does it so "generously!"

When direction is needed, we don't have to take wild shots in the dark and hope for the best. Instead, we can be proactive in our asking, seeking, Bible reading, and listening. We must no longer go about trying to bless others and trying to extinguish church fires based solely on our good intentions, but our efforts must be based on the wisdom that he provides, so that the manner and timing of our efforts are right on target.

If we continue to bless others "loudly" and "in the morning", without seeking direction from God beforehand, then our would-be blessings will sometimes morph into curses, and church fires might grow even larger. Likewise, if we seek God's direction and then refuse to listen to his voice or heed his instructions, our efforts will suffer a similar fate.

The Young Boy and the Elderly Blind Man

While God's Holy Spirit is ready and willing to guide us (John 14:26), we must lend our spiritual ears to him and trust him enough to follow him, even when our natural inclinations might tempt us to do otherwise. When we hesitate to "trust and obey," as the familiar line from the classic hymn reminds us, we can produce curses instead of blessings, and those curses often place us and others in danger of a multitude of negative repercussions. This sort of predicament can be likened to an interesting occurrence between a young boy and an elderly blind man that took place during the great fire that raged within Boston.

An apartment building that was thought to be entirely evacuated of its tenants and was already largely consumed with flames became the center of attention for a large group of bystanders who happened to be gathering on the streets nearby. Some of these bystanders believed they had heard the cries of a young boy coming from within the apartment building, and then their suspicions were confirmed when they observed through a second story window a young boy tugging on the coat of an elderly man, just in front of the landing of the stairway that leads to the ground floor.

This boy and this elderly man had been seen numerous times before by many of those watching the horrific scene unfold that day, as the elderly man was completely blind and had long employed the services of the young boy to be his caretaker. The boy had previously been observed leading the elderly man around town on many occasions.

Immediately after these two individuals were observed to be in the burning building, several men bravely ran toward the main entrance of the apartment building to enter the building and attempt a rescue. They managed to ignore the fear of death and make their way through the heat and smoke and up the stairs to the landing on the second floor. When they arrived, they observed the elderly man stubbornly attempting to go into a blazing room of fire while the young boy was tugging on him with all his might and yelling, "Oh, do, do come out! This is the way! Oh, do come out!"

For whatever reason, the elderly man who had employed the young boy and trusted him in less dangerous circumstances was unwilling to heed the boy's instructions when it mattered the most. Perhaps the intensity of the moment rattled the blind man's ability to think clearly, or perhaps the man stubbornly believed that he somehow knew better how to escape the flames than did the boy who could see exactly where those flames happened to be. In any event, the elderly blind man fought against the young boy's leading, but finally the boy (with the help of the men who had run into the building) was able to drag the elderly blind man to safety, and not a moment too soon. As if the scene was being filmed for a modern-day action movie, the group escaped the apartment building merely seconds before the floors collapsed on each other and the entire building was ablaze. Moments after the escape, bystanders witnessed the teary-eyed young boy emphatically saying to the elderly blind man, "You ought to come with me when I pull you so!"

God no doubt desires each of us to heed this precise piece of advice when it concerns his own pulling and tugging on us, as his Holy Spirit guides us. Like the elderly man in the story, we are often very blind to many factors. On the contrary, God – who is our "Helper" (John 14:26) – knows all things and clearly sees the peril that will befall us and others when we say and do things in the wrong time and in the wrong way. Like the boy in the story, God's Holy Spirit has the duty of guiding the blind within his care. Being figuratively blind of what each circumstance requires of us, we must heed his guidance.

When faced with intense circumstances, such as fires of negativity that are raging within our churches, and wherein we might need to step up and speak or behave in a strategic manner, we must choose to intently listen to God's leading. We must not allow the *heat* of the moment to shake us and throw us off kilter. We must choose to embrace God's leading instead of stubbornly seizing the opportunity for ourselves by rashly making decisions (outside of God's direction) that our figuratively blind eyes aren't equipped to make.

The Fate of Boston's Gas Supply Lines Doesn't Have to Be Repeated

Boston's gas supply lines could have solely been a blessing unto the city, without any of the cursing that took place throughout the duration of the great fire, had they merely been operated in the correct time and in the correct manner. Although these gas lines were intended to bring only positive things into the city, their reputation remains bitter-sweet.

The skewed legacy of Boston's gas supply lines doesn't have to be repeated within us – at least not any longer. As Christ followers, we can ensure that we minister in the right way and in the right time. When dealing with ministry opportunities that come our way or fiery situations within our churches, our words and deeds must be exactly on target. We can say and do the right things in the right time and in the right way – only when we seek God for wisdom and then respond appropriately to his direction, with full trust and obedience.

If you would like to see your church preventing and extinguishing destructive fires, then do your part. Choose to seek God and his guidance before rashly and haphazardly saying and doing things. When God's Holy Spirit pulls and tugs at you to go in a certain direction, trust him enough to immediately obey him, even when doing so is at odds with your own intuition, understanding, and desires. With God leading the way, you can bless others without any fear that those blessings will backfire as curses.

4

Water Power Was Insufficient
Rely on Fresh Power From God

Boston had been forewarned by its Board of Engineers three years prior to the great fire that the financial district of the city was desperately in need of newer and larger water pipes. The Board had also advised that larger reservoirs of water needed to be produced within the vicinity to allow multiple fire engines to extract the water that was needed to battle a large fire, should one occur. Unfortunately, the warnings and advice went unheeded, and Boston did not have the water power it needed to wage an effective war against the raging flames of the great fire.

Boston's small water pipes allowed only two engines to simultaneously pull from the small water reservoirs nearest the financial district, and therefore many engines sat idle or were sent to locations where they were not needed. Moreover, the pressure of the water was not powerful enough to allow firefighters the ability to propel water high enough to combat the fires on the roofs of the buildings, where the fire was spreading rapidly. As firefighters did their best at propelling water as high as the limited pressure would allow, it was as if the roofs of the buildings merely laughed at them. The roofs burned quickly and ferociously, and many remained largely untouched by water.

When it came to propelling water where it was needed, Boston had a power problem. Boston's smaller pipes and smaller reservoirs had sufficed ages ago, when the city and many of its buildings were far smaller. If only Boston had upgraded to larger pipes and larger reservoirs over the years, the fire could have been handled much more efficiently. But instead, the city had decided to rest on its laurels, while believing that its outdated water infrastructure would be sufficient for combating modern fires. Although Boston's fire department had procured some of the newest equipment (such as fire engines, hoses, nozzles, and ladders) prior to the great fire, little good came of these things because of the uphill battle firefighters constantly had to face regarding major deficiencies with their water supply and strength. Unfortunately, Bostonians learned the hard way that power must be fresh and strong, because modern fires don't care about the power that existed previously, nor are they intimidated by yesterday's firefighting successes.

Power is Often in Short Supply Within the Church

Many fires begin and rage within many of God's churches today because a number of church members (sometimes entire congregations) aren't operating with fresh power from on high, and they therefore can't combat fires effectively. When the power of God isn't operating from within church members, negative church fires have the potential to figuratively burn an entire church to the ground. Moreover, after these fires have destroyed a church, its congregants (like embers) often go into other churches and carry the same kind of fires into them, thus starting new fires that have the potential to burn down additional churches, if there's no firefighting power operating from within the members of those churches.

Powerless individuals within a church are reminiscent of individuals who were seen hopelessly watching their Bostonian businesses and houses burn to the ground while being able to do absolutely nothing to combat the fire. In one sad scene, people were observed to be giving away everything that belonged to them as quickly as possible to bystanders on the streets. These individuals chose to see precious family heirlooms, expensive clothes, and many other items given to strangers instead of watching them go up in smoke. Priests and other workers at a Catholic church that was rapidly being destroyed by the fire were seen throwing religious art, costly imported items, crucifixes, priestly ornaments, and much more into the hands of hundreds of bystanders and then urging them to take them and flee. And it's just like this within churches today when church members aren't sufficiently powerful in Christ to combat negative church fires; the hands of an all-too-eager Satan are there to grab hold of everything of value that was once exclusively meant to be a blessing within these various churches.

Individuals who want to see negative church fires

prevented or snuffed out before the worst of calamities occurs must be full of the Holy Spirit and freshly walking in his power. God's Word makes this abundantly clear. For instance, when the early church faced a negative church fire regarding a group of widows being overlooked during the ministry of food distributions, the apostles explained that the men chosen to extinguish this fire were to be "full of the Spirit" (Acts 6:3). In other words, they had to be individuals who were not content with seeing church fires grow to destroy what God was up to, but they had to have within them a deep reservoir of fresh power from the Holy Spirit that would allow them to combat the problems that threatened the ministry. Likewise, today's churches need to be composed of people who are full of the Holy Spirit's power and ready to fight the fires that threaten what God is doing within those churches.

Some Individuals are Powerless Because They Don't Have the Power Supply

Many church members are unable to effectively wage war on negative church fires because God's power isn't operating from within them, and it never has. Merely going to church and being somewhat active within the church community does not make an individual a bona fide follower of Christ. Only when an individual puts a genuine trust in Jesus Christ does he truly belong to Christ, and only then is there access to the reservoir of power that is made available to believers by way of the Holy Spirit, who resides within each Christ follower.

During the onset of the early church, seven brothers learned the hard way that God's power was not something that could merely be summoned. They learned that God's reservoir of power first had to reside within an individual (belonging to God) before it could then be manifested through him (Acts 19:11-20). While these seven brothers had never been indwelled with God's Holy Spirit, they nevertheless believed they could summon God's power at-will. Because their father was a Jewish High Priest, and because they believed they were well versed in the vernacular of real Christ followers, these brothers believed they could send God's power where it needed to be. Therefore, on one occasion, these seven brothers attempted to gang up (as would-be firefighters) on a man who was possessed by an evil spirit. Despite their best efforts to summon God's power with the use of various words they had heard used by others, the man with the evil spirit was unfazed, due to their absolute lack of power. In fact, the evil spirit from within the man spoke through his victim, as if amused by the men's bravado, and said, "Jesus, I know, and Paul I recognize, but who are *you*?" Before giving the ineffectual brothers time to respond, the man with the evil spirit began to physically attack all seven brothers at once. He beat them senseless, tore off their clothes, and forced them to run away naked and bloody.

Just like these seven brothers, there are individuals within God's churches who don't belong to Christ but who nevertheless believe they can aid in firefighting efforts. Perhaps it's their church attendance, familial relationships with well-known people inside or outside the church, their ability to temporarily imitate true Christ followers in words and deeds, or any number of other factors that give them a false sense of access to power that is entirely unavailable to them. Regardless, their attempts to fight fires within God's churches never prevail, and they often make fires worse!

Conversely, those who know Christ for themselves and truly belong to him have received power (1 Timothy 1:7) and can minister boldly and effectively as they extinguish fires that come along. Each true Christ follower can draw from the reservoir of power that resides within him, due to the indwelling of God's Holy Spirit, and then he can take appropriate firefighting actions. This fact does not mean that Christ followers always utilize the power that is at their disposal, but the power to fight fires without getting whipped is nevertheless available.

If you're a church member (or attender) who does not belong to Christ and are therefore powerless to help fight negative fires within your church, there's hope. You don't have to remain powerless. More importantly, you don't have to remain separated from God with a debt of sin that you can never repay on your own. By trusting in Jesus Christ, regarding the good news concerning his death, burial, and resurrection, you can belong to Christ and live with God forever, even after your physical life ends on this earth. As a bonus, firefighting power will become available to you even before you step into eternity, so you will be able to work alongside your fellow Christ followers in extinguishing and preventing fires within your church. You can learn more about this "good news" by reading the addendum chapter (page 105) entitled, "Euchred, Pard!" This chapter is written especially for those who are not yet Christ followers, and it begins with an interesting story about soldiers who were ordered to keep people out of certain areas of Boston in the days just after the great fire.

Some Individuals Are Powerless Because They're More Interested in Power-Talking Than Power-Walking

Just because God's firefighting power is available to genuine Christ followers doesn't mean that all Christ followers make use of it. Sadly, some individuals are more content with *talking* about God's power than *walking* consistently in his power. Some individuals (and sometimes, entire church congregations) like to talk about power as if it only existed in the past or as if it will only exist at some point in the future. The former is always talking about the "good ole' days", when God did mighty works through them or their church, and the latter is always talking about what God is going to do through them or their church – one sweet day. Sadly, it's like these individuals and churches have forgotten that God's power is available to them *now*, and this is why their firefighting efforts are always merely discussed and never deployed.

God does not want those who belong to him to be talkers but walkers, actively walking in his power on a continuous basis. The Apostle Paul made this clear when he addressed a group of Christ followers who had earned the reputation of being boastful and arrogant (1 Corinthians 4:16-21). These individuals had made a habit of merely *talking* about themselves and others, and Paul wrote to them and demanded that they start *walking* (living) in power, just as he did. He then warned them that he hoped to soon visit them, in order that he might be able to see for himself if they were truly walking in power or merely continuing to run their mouths. He taught them that "the kingdom of God does not consist in talk but in power," and he asked them if he was going to need to treat them like little children when he finally came and laid eyes on them, regarding having to scold them if their walking was not far surpassing their talking. Paul then challenged these individuals to step up and utilize the power that was available to them, in order to fight a monstrous fire of negativity that had been allowed to rise up within their church (1 Corinthians 5:1-13), and he reminded them that they could do exactly what they needed to do "with the power of the Lord Jesus!"

Likewise, God wants those who belong to him today to realize that his kingdom operates and advances with power, rather than a bunch of talking. Power is the driving force. Christ followers must stop boasting about the past or what might happen in the future and start living lives of power right now, especially if modern church fires are to be prevented or extinguished before they destroy churches completely.

If your life as a Christ follower has recently been more about talking than walking and living in God's power, make a change! Begin to engross yourself in God's Word more than you ever have before. As you read his Word, begin making note of what God has called you to do, and then get to work! Begin walking in his power daily, and let your actions replace the talking in which you may have once engaged. Consistently choose to "keep in step with God's Spirit" (Galatians 5:25), and thus begin helping to prevent and extinguish fires within your church!

Some Individuals Are Powerless Because They Have Rust in Their Pipes

Years before the great fire, Boston's Fire Chief John Damrell had discovered that some of Boston's water mains had begun to rust and corrode, reducing the diameter for water flow from six inches to nearly four inches in some areas. Damrell had implored the town council to approve of a measure that would replace these pipes with eight-inch pipes that would allow a steady flow of water for firefighting purposes, but they had repeatedly brushed him off and told him that he was being too extravagant in his requests. As a result, the rusted and corroded water pipes played a huge role in minimizing the water power that was needed to fight the fire.

In a similar way, some Christ followers can't fight negative church fires with power at full force because their pipes have become rusty and clogged by their sinful lifestyles. When Christ followers choose to indulge their sinful desires instead of fighting them at every turn, God's love for them does not diminish, but the Holy Spirit's ability to work through them certainly does. Take a Christ follower's prayers, for example: God's Word says that "the prayer of a righteous person has great power" (James 5:16), while the prayer of someone who consistently surrenders to sin is powerless (1 Peter 3:12). Habitual and controlling sins have such a devastating effect on those who choose to give their sins a pass instead of annihilating them. Like clogged pipes, these individuals can't possibly be used to fight fires at full force.

God's Word beckons Christ followers to replace pipes that have been clogged by the rust of habitual sins with clean pipes that allow his power to flow freely from within. Christ followers are instructed to "lay aside every weight and sin that clings so closely" (Hebrews 12:1) and to strive to live holy in every manner of conduct and in total opposition to former lifestyles that were once lived apart from him (1 Peter 1:14-15).

Replacing clogged pipes isn't easy. Just as Damrell was told that his desire for new pipes was an extravagant request, you need to know that any clogged and sinful pipes of your own that need replacing will require a lot of work. God's Word challenges Christ followers to rise to the occasion and "put to death" (or assassinate) everything that is sinful within them (Colossians 3:5). These extreme measures require total and consistent commitment, and they aren't to be performed only once. Defeating sin is a war that is waged over a lifetime, as clean and holy living remains the constant goal.

If you're a Christ follower who is lacking in power, begin battling your sin today and *every* day for the rest of your life. Don't let clogged and sinful pipes of your life keep you from honoring God with holy conduct, and don't let your sins prevent you from effectively fighting negative church fires. Take a page out of the playbook of the Apostle Paul: constantly make war against your sinful habits, and strive to keep the pipes of your life clean and under control at all times (1 Corinthians 9:26-27). Only then can you begin to powerfully help extinguish and prevent fires within your church.

A Special Prayer for Power

The Apostle Paul not only constantly fought his own sin and instructed others to do likewise, he prayed a specific prayer for all Christ followers – that God "may grant you to be strengthened with power through his Spirit in your inner being" (Ephesians 3:16). Fighting church fires can be done successfully rather than in futility! God's work within your church can move forward when you and other Christ followers are ministering in full force, with fresh power from the Spirit of God! But the news gets even better, for Paul ended his prayer in this way: "Now to him who is able to do far more abundantly than all we ask or think, according to the power at work within us, to him be the glory in the church and in Christ Jesus throughout all generations, forever and ever. Amen" (Ephesians 3:20-21). In other words, God will often bring blessings and firefighting successes that are larger than anyone could have imagined, "according to the power at work within us" – *his* power!

Therefore, belong to Christ and have his power supply within you. Be a power-walker instead of a power-talker. Always strive to keep your pipes clean from the rust of sin. Do these things, and then watch God make Paul's prayer applicable to you. Your church will be much safer for it!

5

Instructions from the Expert Were Not Heeded
Make God's Word Preeminent in All Situations

Prior to the great fire, Bostonians had gone about building their homes, apartments, and businesses however they saw fit. There were no fire codes or fire-preventative building regulations in place. Even though several smaller fires had occurred in Boston over the years prior to the great fire, there had been little effort on behalf of city officials and property owners to change their building practices to avoid similar fires, let alone a monstrous fire.

On the other hand, there was Boston's Fire Chief John Damrell, an expert in fire prevention. Damrell had spent years studying fires by traveling to other places after major fires had occurred. For years, he had petitioned Boston's city officials to enforce a variety of regulations that would better equip Boston to withstand a major fire. Damrell was particularly concerned with Boston's narrow streets, its very tall buildings, and its lack of water power due to old and rusted water pipes. However, prior to the great fire, most of Damrell's pleas had gone unheeded. City officials had repeatedly charged Damrell, the only true fire expert among them, with being too aggressive in his endeavors to safeguard the city from fire.

Nevertheless, the city attempted to appease Damrell by way of enforcing mandatory fire inspections of city buildings. They also commissioned the construction of a fire boat. However, the fire inspections hardly paid off, as building owners were under no compulsion to act on the instructions of the fire department. The fire boat, which would have aided firefighters immensely by allowing them to propel water from the harbor into various areas of Boston's financial district during the great fire, was not completed and deployed until a year after the great fire.

If only Boston had elected to follow the advice of its fire expert before the great fire had begun, most assuredly the fire wouldn't have been nearly as catastrophic upon the city. For starters, the roofs of new buildings would have been constructed with fire-repellant materials instead of materials that embers could so easily ignite, dry storage goods within various businesses would have been stored more properly, and the city's water mains would have been replaced with new and larger pipes, allowing firefighters the needed water power to effectively combat the great fire. Sadly, only in the aftermath of the great fire did Boston realize its colossal mistake in refusing to honor the instructions of its expert, Fire Chief Damrell. Of course, by then it was too late.

Sometimes Churches Fail to Heed Our Expert's Instructions

Unfortunately, churches are sometimes built (regarding their practices and procedures) with little or no regard for the instructions of the church-building expert, God. Just as Damrell knew how to safeguard a city from a disastrous fire and thus warned and petitioned Boston to respond appropriately to his instructions, God is the only one who truly knows exactly how his church should operate. God has given us his Word (the Bible) to show each of us how we can go about building and protecting churches *his* way. His divine expertise, revealed to us by way of many biblical authors, is in fact "breathed out" (or generated) by him. That expertise is "profitable for teaching, for reproof, for correction, and for training in righteousness" (2 Timothy 3:16), in order that each of us might partake in building and participating within churches in a way that isn't conducive to negative fires that would try to destroy God's work. And yet, some Christ followers remain oblivious to God's instructions, or they occasionally ignore or reject his instructions (most specifically, the instructions that they don't prefer) in order that they may behave within a church as *they* deem necessary. These Christ followers will make decisions and establish protocols based on their own faulty judgements and ideas rather than following the ironclad instructions of our only expert, God.

When Christ followers go about deciding how God's church will operate, they're basically ignoring God while proclaiming that his fire codes are merely suggestive and not authoritative. All the while, his Word regularly warns us to do the exact opposite: "Trust in the LORD with all your heart, and do not lean on your own understanding" (Proverbs 3:5). "Be doers of the word, and not hearers only" (James 1:22).

Nevertheless, some Christ followers are content with merely trying to appease God. They somehow believe that if they act appropriately regarding a couple of God's instructions, they can go in a different direction concerning the rest. When a church has too many of these thinkers in its midst, especially when this warped philosophy exists within the hearts and minds of even a small percentage of a church's leadership, church fires are bound to occur, and the devastation is always extreme. When church fires happen, individuals are often deeply hurt, churches often fold or split, and Satan occasionally succeeds in convincing some individuals to put a permanent end to their church involvement altogether. And yet, most of these fires could likely be avoided if only God's instructions, set forth within his Word, were appropriately esteemed and practiced by all.

Fire Codes Require Great Effort to Follow, But the Payoff is Worth It

The city of Boston was unwilling to follow the sage instructions of its expert, Fire Chief Damrell, because doing so would have required a great deal of effort, not to mention the financial costs. For example, updating poorly built buildings and constructing newer buildings with a dogged fixation on meeting rigid fire codes and keeping to building regulations is a great deal more difficult than simply leaving poorly built buildings as they are and building newer buildings with no restrictions or guidelines. And yet, the effort could have saved Bostonians from a lot of grief in the end.

The same is true of God's building instructions for us. Following the instructions of our only expert requires great effort on behalf of each of us, but the long-term benefits include having healthy individuals who make up healthy and relatively fireproof churches. It isn't easy to follow God's instructions, especially when poor building practices have already taken place, but for individuals and churches who choose to make God's Word preeminent in all matters of practice and procedure, a fireproofing of sorts will be the result.

For instance, consider God's fire code regarding how an individual within a church should respond when someone else in the church has mistreated him and refuses to make amends (Matthew 18:15-17). God's Word outlines a protocol of procedures that can sometimes be difficult, embarrassing, time consuming, and frustrating. First, the mistreated individual should go to his fellow Christ follower and talk things over privately with him. If the offending party refuses to make amends, the mistreated individual should approach the offending party a second time along with one or two other Christ followers who might serve to act as mediators. If this strategy fails to bring reconciliation between the two individuals, leaders of the church should be informed of the situation and then trusted to make judgements and corrections concerning the matter. Finally, if the offending party refuses to listen to the correction of church leaders, the mistreated individual should distance himself from the offending party and have no interaction with the offender going forward.

While this plain and methodical fire code comes not only from God's Word, but straight from the mouth of Jesus, many individuals and churches pay no attention to it. Instead, some take matters into their own hands; they complain, gossip, pick fights, entice others to form sides, leave churches, and more. They opt for what's easiest and most gratifying to their selfish desires. They go about shaping the practices and procedures within their church, and sadly, the rest of the congregation and its leaders may not try to stop them. And thus, raging fires take their course – all because God's fire code was unheeded and nobody was willing to put forth great effort to see that it was followed. As fires between Christ followers begin to rage over individuals who have wronged one another, the blessings that come only from following our expert's instructions aren't realized.

This fire code is just one example of many. God's Word addresses a multitude of issues regarding how to formulate proper practices and procedures within his church, but each of us as Christ followers must be willing to heed our expert's instructions and work hard to employ them, both individually and corporately. We should strive for a culture within our churches that consistently heralds God's Word as preeminent at all times and regarding all things. God's fire codes concerning how pastors are to preach, leaders are to be chosen, and abilities (or gifts) are to be used are found in God's Word, and his Word contains many other fire codes that likewise address building procedures of huge importance. When these fire codes are eagerly received as authoritative rather than suggestive, a church will have far fewer fires, and the few fires that happen to pop up on occasion will be snuffed out much more quickly!

Stay Out of the Sewer

When a Christ follower chooses to follow his own path within a church, even after having read or been taught the proper building procedures established by our expert, he will often come to regret it in the worst and most embarrassing ways. His only recourse will be to depend on the hands of the expert, whose instructions had previously been ignored, to rescue him from a colossal mess.

Similar was the case for a couple of young men who were relic hunting in the weeks after the great fire. Having found ways to sneak past various military guards who had been stationed to keep people out of certain areas, the two young men were on the prowl for interesting items that they could collect and later sell to others who were willing to pay large sums of money for items that showcased the wear and tear of the historic fire.

On one occasion, the two well-dressed young men happened upon a construction area and noticed that several burnt timbers had been strategically placed over an excavation site. As they attempted to investigate, a couple of construction workers took notice of the young men and ordered them to immediately "clear out." At that moment, the young men had little choice but to follow the instructions of the construction workers. As they left the area, the young men discussed with one another their strong belief that something of great importance just *had* to be underneath the timbers, and it was moments later that that the young men ventured back to the scene.

Ignoring the instructions of the construction workers, and working to remain undetected by them on this go-around, the young men secretly but quickly advanced toward the area blockaded by the timbers. Upon reaching their destination, the young men fell into a sewer with a loud crash; they had been moving too quickly to prevent themselves from the fall. Disappointed and humiliated, the young men couldn't manage to escape the sewer on their own, and their plight was observed by the very two construction workers who had earlier instructed them to stay away from the area. As the construction workers helped pull the young men out of the sewer, the young men most likely had one prevailing thought on their minds: "Too bad we didn't listen to the experts!"

Similarly, there are countless Christ followers who have found themselves in figurative sewers because they have opted to ignore God's instructions and to follow their own plans and desires. When individuals find themselves in a mess like this, there are two things that must be done. First, confess your poor decisions to God, and allow him to help you out of the sewer. He will forgive you for ignoring his instructions and choosing your own path (1 John 1:9). Though you may suffer embarrassment and pain in the aftermath of your decisions, he won't allow you to forever-remain stuck in your despair. Second, vigorously endeavor to follow God's instructions from this moment forward, and if applicable, you can start by following the very instructions that would have prevented your sewer mishaps in the first place. You can bet the young men who were rescued from their literal sewer with their filthy clothes and their bruised egos immediately chose to permanently vacate the premises!

If Reconstruction is Necessary, Begin With God's Fire Codes at the Forefront

When entire church bodies have suffered an array of negative and devastating fires because God's fire codes have been ignored, reconstruction must take place just as it did in Boston after the great fire. Boston began to heed the instructions of their only expert, Fire Chief Damrell, and the city began to rebuild in a manner conducive to fire prevention. Fire codes of all kinds were adopted and enforced, and the city was safer for it. Likewise, God's churches must choose to rebuild with God's Word at the forefront.

However, there are some congregations that may believe the destruction within their churches has simply been too immense for any possibility of recovery. Because of this, some members might propose that efforts to rebuild, albeit with a determination to adhere to God's fire codes, would nevertheless be an act of futility. They might suggest that shutting the doors to the church altogether is the only remaining option. But this is hardly the case if a large percentage of the church is determined to scrap the faulty measures of the past and rebuild with God's Word as the blueprint.

When a church has been tormented by one fire after another, it can start afresh and build on top of the wreckage. Boston's financial district grew significantly in real estate as the remnants of burned buildings were pushed into the harbor. Extending hundreds of feet in some areas, the wreckage was used as foundations for new buildings that would have stood in the ocean had they been built before the great fire. Within a couple of years, Boston had many more new buildings than the number of buildings that had been destroyed, and because the city was moving forward in all areas with newly adopted fire codes, Boston eventually grew into a bigger, better, and stronger city than anyone could have imagined. The same can be true of your church! Before shutting the doors on a church and tossing all hope to the wind, ask God to help your church start afresh. If God chooses to spare your church from absolute calamity, thank him and begin to build over the remnants of negative fires with God's instructions at the forefront.

As your church begins to follow God's fire codes, God may require your church to reevaluate everything about your church. Your church might be led to change bylaws, procedures, programs, values, teachings, and even missional statements. When God's Word is made the blue print for rebuilding efforts, any number of changes may be on the horizon. But have no fear! If your church consists largely of individuals who are dedicated to following the instructions of the expert, even the biggest changes can be accomplished, and your church will be much better for it. Your church might be a smoky, burned-out mess right now, but it will be better and stronger than ever down the road. God's power and glory manifested within your church can be unparalleled when his instructions are stringently followed like never before!

Every Area of Your Life Should be Saturated With God's Fire Codes

The Apostle Paul instructed each Christ follower to "let the word of Christ dwell in you richly" (Colossians 3:16). This means that every area of our lives should be saturated with God's Word, and then we can do the things that Paul talked about next. We can teach and admonish others correctly, we can sing the right kind of songs, we can thank God appropriately and sincerely, and everything else we do "in word or deed" can be done "in the name of the Lord Jesus," including preventing and extinguishing negative fires within our churches (Colossians 3:16-17).

If you haven't done so already, begin to engross yourself in God's Word and soak up his fire codes. Hide them in your heart, as did David (Psalm 119:11), and then endeavor to follow his codes in every area of your life. Encourage fellow Christ followers to do likewise, and pray for your church – that God's Word will be preeminent in all things. In these ways, you will make extraordinary advances toward the fireproofing of your church.

6

Looting Was Rampant
Never Seek to Personally Benefit from Negativity

Many Bostonians probably thought things couldn't get any worse during the first few hours of the fire. As hundreds of buildings were burning to the ground, some individuals witnessed their homes or businesses destroyed before their very eyes, while others frantically did whatever they could do to salvage family heirlooms, important documents, and other invaluable items before the fire swept them up. Nevertheless, things *did* get worse. As if Boston didn't already have enough troubles on its plate while combating the great fire, hundreds of individuals chose to compound Boston's problems by looting from stores and homes during the fiery melee.

The selfishness of these looting Bostonians knew no bounds. They were grabbing anything and everything that they could get their hands on and then taking off, as they used the misfortune of thousands of fellow Bostonians for their own gain. So many looters filled the fire-threatened buildings that firefighters often found it extremely difficult to enter various buildings to fight the fire. While police officers were arresting looters through the night (hundreds within the first couple of hours), other looters remained undeterred, as they continued to take advantage of Boston's terrible circumstances for their own illegal gain.

Some individuals brazenly stole personal items from people right in front of them. They unabashedly swiped items from collections on the streets and sidewalks, where families and business owners were trying to stand-guard and protect the few items they had managed to salvage from the fire. Still, there were other Bostonians who couldn't bring themselves to rob their fellow citizens outright, but they nevertheless chose a more legal looting strategy: they charged desperate individuals a small fortune to lend a hand and help carry precious items to a safer location. It was an absolute free-for-all for those who wanted to profit off of Boston's terrible predicament, and sadly, many individuals chose to do just that.

Among those individuals included a handful of firemen, servants of the city who had sworn to protect Boston in the face of tragedy. Despite their allegiances to the city, these firemen were seen taking personal items from stores and homes after entering those buildings for firefighting purposes. In fact, in the days following the fire, several firemen were overheard lamenting with one another about having been unable to get their share of the spoils during the fire because other looters had beat them to the goods before the firemen had arrived. Indeed, a few firemen were among the number of those who were caught looting and then arrested by police officers. Boston's terrible and painful circumstances had truly brought out the vultures within some individuals. For them, their desire and willingness to loot and take advantage of others was more compelling than helping others during the travesty that Boston was facing. For them, personal gain trumped any compulsion they may have had to help protect the city they called home.

There are Looters in Every Church

When fires of negativity occur within God's churches, there are always individuals who immediately take notice and then go about trying to capitalize on the grim circumstances. Most notorious are the gossips, individuals who rush to share details about a negative fire they've witnessed (or heard about from fellow gossips) to either a select group of people or to anyone willing to listen. Rather than choosing to selflessly help extinguish a fire, gossips choose to selfishly loot the situation by making it a means by which they can obtain a cheap and fleeting thrill. Gossips would rather spew the details of a fiery situation to others than lift a finger to help extinguish the fire. To make matters worse, the details they share are often laced with exaggerations or blatant inaccuracies, as gossips rarely care about getting the facts straight. Like looters, gossips merely want a quick and easy reward, and they'll use a fiery situation for their own gain in a heartbeat, no matter the harm their looting brings to others.

Gossips will loot a negative situation for everything it's worth. Some of them even become braggarts who gossip about the shortcomings of others, so they can portray themselves as superior and holier. As they look down their noses at those who have started or propagated a church fire, these gossips walk around with their looted spoils of pride and arrogance. Still, others will try to gossip and boast their way into positions of power within a church, and they'll use a church fire as fuel for their power plays. Because of reasons such as these, negative fires within a church are not only welcomed by looters with open arms, they're often started by gossips in the first place.

For clarification, the sin and heinous nature of looting gossips within a church is not necessarily the telling of information. Sometimes accurate information (even when damaging, painful, and embarrassing to some) must be *appropriately* shared with others, so that the processes of biblical correction, warning, and restoration may be allowed to take place. What differentiates those who appropriately pass along necessary information and those who gossip is both a matter of the heart and of protocol. For instance, if the heart of one disseminating fiery information to others is at all seeking any kind of personal gain, that person is a gossip who is looting a negative situation for his own selfish purposes. Conversely, the heart of an individual who appropriately shares information is genuinely grieved and hurting about the necessity to share; it's often embarrassing and uncomfortable for the person to share what he wishes were not true. Moreover, as a matter of protocol, an individual who appropriately shares information will only do so when he is personally unable to extinguish a fire himself (after exhausting his own firefighting abilities), and those with whom he shares information will only be those who are able to do more than him in combating the fire. Meanwhile, a gossip will refuse to personally partake in firefighting efforts and will generally spread information to others who either likewise refuse to partake in firefighting efforts or are unable to do anything productive even if they wanted to help.

Gossips are in just about every church, and their truest desires are to benefit themselves over and above counting others "more significant" than themselves (Philippians 2:3). Gossips will selfishly loot a negative church fire long before they'll ever do anything to "encourage one another" or "build one another up," (1 Thessalonians 5:11) because the former is easy and offers an immediate thrill, while the latter takes effort and requires personal sacrifice.

Don't Be a Ham

While God's Word contains several passages that warn against those who loot by way of gossiping, perhaps one of the most powerful passages regarding the matter can be found in the story of Ham (Genesis 9:18-27). The story begins with Ham's father, Noah, who planted a vineyard and began to drink of its wine. Unfortunately, Noah drank enough wine to become drunk. At some point, he passed out in the nude within his own tent. Ham was the first person to happen upon the embarrassing situation and notice his father's drunken stupor, and Ham immediately faced a choice.

With his father's reputation on the line, not to mention the shame such an event would cause Ham's entire family, Ham could have chosen to act in a way that would have protected the dignity of his father and his family. For instance, he could have covered his father's nakedness, said nothing of the matter to anyone else, and then (later) privately addressed his sober father regarding the imprudent predicament that he had caused for himself, so that his father might heed the wise and gentle warning and never allow a similar situation to happen again. Or perhaps Ham could have merely exited his father's tent and remained on-watch for a while, to keep others from entering the tent, before later addressing his father privately. Regardless, Ham's choice could have been selfless, and his actions could have snuffed out a fire and minimized the damage. While such a choice would not have been immediately advantageous to Ham, as it would have required personal sacrifice (regarding the time and effort involved), Ham could have chosen to do what was necessary to protect his father and his family.

Alternatively, Ham chose to selfishly loot the situation for his own gain. In fact, no sooner than Ham's eyes had spotted his father in an awful predicament, Ham's mouth was ready to gossip about the details to anyone willing to listen. Those first to hear Ham's report were his two brothers, and they were first only because they were closest to him (just outside the tent). Ham craved the cheap thrill that gossiping provided more than he cared about sacrificially protecting his own family, and thus he took advantage of his father's self-made fire and victimized his two brothers in the process, in as much as he used them as recipients of his gossip. While Ham could have extinguished a threatening fire within his family, he selfishly chose to exacerbate the fire instead.

God doesn't want us to be Hams within our church families. In fact, the Apostle Paul revealed God's views on the matter when he described gossips as deserving of God's wrath, and Paul further chastised them by throwing them in the company of "murderers" and "haters of God," deserving severe punishment (Romans 1:18-32). Instead of behaving like Ham when we encounter a fire within our church families, we can choose to behave like Ham's two brothers! – Upon witnessing Ham's ill-treatment of their father's plight, Shem and Japheth walked backward into their father's tent and covered their father's nakedness. They weren't seeking personal gain; they were instead seeking to benefit their entire family by sacrificially doing the right thing.

God wants us to behave as did Ham's brothers when we observe a fire within our church families. In other words, we are to sacrificially do the work of damage-minimalization and fire extinguishing when we have the means – and when we can do so in an appropriate manner. Regarding occasions wherein we may be unable to do these things, we must be sure to share information about a church fire only with those who can do more than we can do. While sharing, if it comes to that, our hearts should genuinely be grief-stricken in the process. The damage of a church fire is nothing to rejoice or gloat about, unless you're a looter.

Looters Always Lose

Those who are willing to loot within their church families for personal gain may walk around with smiles on their faces for a season, but they never stay happy for too long. There's only so much temporary pride and contentment one can achieve after each gossip session (even if he is able to gossip his way into a powerplay of sorts) before the looter must search-out or start another church fire in hopes of another fresh hit of spoils. Like a drug addict, looters are always looking for more opportunities to serve themselves, but what they never seem to understand is that they're constantly making matters worse for themselves (not just others) each time they loot.

Aside from sowing divisions and losing friends (Proverbs 16:28), gossips invite curses upon themselves when they loot negative situations within their church families. The Apostle Paul, when referring to young widows who were "going about from house to house" as "gossips and busybodies, saying what they should not", described this kind of looting as straying "after Satan" (1 Timothy 5:13-15). When a person chooses to loot, God's blessings are often prevented, as God's wrath and judgment are invited upon one who has succumbed to what God's Word defines as satanic activity.

Ham invited his own curses when he chose to gossip about his father's bad move and the poor predicament that followed. When Noah had sobered up and learned what Ham had done, Noah cursed Ham in one of the worst ways possible – by declaring that Ham's brothers would be blessed richly by God while

Ham's own son, Canaan, would serve as a slave. This of course was a curse not just on Ham as an individual, but on his legacy and family line (Genesis 9:24-27). Two of the things that Ham probably considered to be of utmost importance were tainted because of his decision to gossip. Similarly, those who choose to gossip in God's churches today often find critical and important pieces of their lives cursed and crumbling. Because we have a Heavenly Father who can't stand to see his children behaving selfishly and deviously, he allows those who sow evil to reap corruption within their lives (Galatians 6:7-8).

Sowing and reaping was a lesson learned rather swiftly by one particular looter on the day of the great fire. This looter was a teamster who transported goods in his own cart for a living, and he had offered a desperate business owner his services regarding moving the man's dry goods two blocks away from the fire. When the cart had been fully loaded, the teamster then demanded that the man immediately give him seventy-five dollars in cash, on the spot, before he would budge. The exorbitant amount was unpayable, and the business owner angrily left the scene. The teamster then took the man's dry goods to his own home, and he was arrested the next morning and placed in jail. Would you believe it? – This looter was charged a fine of *seventy-five dollars* to be released! Indeed, looters always lose, eventually. The law of reaping and sowing always runs its course, and this principle remains consistently true regarding those who gossip within God's churches.

Walk Backward

If you want to help your church extinguish negative fires before they grow out of control and cause great damage, don't be a gossip. God's Word teaches that gossips only add fuel to negative fires, while problems are minimized when gossips aren't around (Proverbs 26:20). As we've discussed, Ham (whose Hebrew name literally means "hot") added fuel to the fire and made things even *hotter* when he happened upon a negative situation and then chose to gossip about it instead of selflessly doing the right thing. This kind of looting can burden, damage, or destroy a church that is unprepared to extinguish its fires and discipline its looters.

In addition to keeping yourself from becoming a looter, stay far away from those who have chosen to do just the opposite. God's Word instructs those of us wanting to fireproof our churches not to associate with gossips (Proverbs 20:19). When you can, you are to avoid those who cause division and serve their own appetites (Romans 16:17-18). If a looter approaches you and immediately begins to use you as a recipient of his gossip, choose not to partake. You don't have to remain an unwilling participant; you can immediately take steps to shut down the nasty dynamics of the conversation, or you can flee the presence of the looter altogether.

Finally, when there's a negative situation that falls upon you to extinguish, selflessly act in a swift and appropriate manner to minimize damage and extinguish the fire. All the while, make sure to "walk backward" toward the situation, as did Ham's brothers (Genesis

9:23). In other words, take selfless and sacrificial steps to prevent yourself from making negative situations worse. Walking backward toward negative fires within your church means that you're constantly seeking to honor others as much as you possibly can (Romans 12:10), and it also means that you're doing whatever it takes to prevent yourself from succumbing to the temptation to capitalize on the plight of others. Walking backward toward negative fires helps you keep your hands (and your heart) clean, as you humbly endeavor to extinguish church fires without getting caught up in a fire of your own (Galatians 6:1). When you do these things, both you and your church will be blessed, and negative church fires will be more easily extinguished!

7

Bystanders Were Everywhere
Do Something or Get Out of the Way

During one of Boston's most trying circumstances, as thousands of home owners and business owners were frantically and laboriously trying to save as much as possible from a fiery doom, tens of thousands of other Bostonians filled the streets merely to watch the devastation of the great fire occur before their very eyes. Most of these bystanders were Bostonians whose homes and businesses were not directly in harm's way, at least not early on, and so they quickly flooded the streets in Boston's financial district to gaze upon the plight of others.

Some of these bystanders were in fact those who had already watched their own properties destroyed by the fire, and they unfortunately had no place else to immediately go and therefore nothing else to immediately do, aside from standing and watching others face the same misfortune they had faced. And yet there were others (by the thousands) in areas surrounding Boston who learned of the fire and hastily made their voyage to the burning city to stand in awestruck amazement at the sites of the atrocity. Many even came by boat and train from neighboring states, as newspaper stories and images in the hours and days that followed only whetted their appetites to view the enormous damage trail of the great fire with their own eyes.

Unfortunately, the magnitude of bystanders that gathered in the streets during the fire made it extremely difficult for firefighters to do their jobs. It was very difficult to get fire engines where they needed to be, and firefighters had to slowly sift through crowds of people to get in and out of burning buildings. Police officers were also impeded at performing their duties, as many looters were made undetectable and hidden by the large crowds of bystanders within the streets. Most bystanders were not willing to move when instructed to do so by the officers, because there were far too many bystanders present to be arrested for not complying.

If only bystanders had done something helpful or merely stayed out of the way of those who were vigorously trying to extinguish the fire, the fire wouldn't have been nearly as destructive. Firefighters, police officers, city officials, and others could have performed their duties far more efficiently, and the city would have been far better off because of it. But the captivating appeal of watching a negative situation happen in real time propelled thousands of individuals to perhaps unintentionally hinder and thwart firefighting efforts. A large portion of Boston burned to the ground, and there were those who merely stood by and watched it happen, as they did absolutely nothing to help extinguish the fire.

Churches are Often Full of Bystanders

When fiery situations are taking place within a church, especially if the negativity is playing out on a public scale, bystanders will almost always be located strategically around the epicenter of the ongoing destruction. These bystanders may love the church and feel deeply saddened to witness negativity within the church, but because they believe themselves to be powerless to improve matters (or clueless as to how they might help), they will choose to watch a fire take place before their very eyes, while they do nothing.

Other individuals who might be somewhat far-removed from a negative situation within a church will sometimes inject themselves into the viewing party. Just as Boston had bystanders from different cities and states come to gawk at its terrible circumstances, churches are often inundated with outsiders who become bystanders and gawkers during a public church fire. These bystanders are those who either have never had an official connection with the church or haven't been active within the church in a long time. During a church fire, these bystanders will sometimes show up to services, business meetings, and other public gatherings of the church to observe negativity with their own eyes. Most of the time, these bystanders will either watch and do nothing constructive, or they'll succumb to enticements to loot and use the fire for their own purposes (to gossip, grumble, make power plays, or add fuel to the fire in other ways).

When bystanders pack the scene, while others are legitimately at work trying to appropriately extinguish fires, a congestion of sorts takes place. There is a slowing down of firefighting efforts. When individuals inject themselves into the fray of negativity just to watch the outcome, church leaders and others who are working to resolve conflict and to protect the church from damage must devote much of their focus trying to decipher *who* is involved in *what*. Problems only compound when bystanders become looters and others become self-appointed supervisors. Some of these supervisors will go about telling firefighters how to minister affectively, while they aren't willing to lift a finger themselves. When too many bystanders insert themselves where they don't belong, negative church fires grow harder to extinguish, and additional fires often spring up.

Don't Just Stand There – Do Something!

When a church fire is blazing and you're one of the witnesses, don't just stand by and watch, while making matters worse. Do *something* to help extinguish the fire and minimize the damage. If you belong to God, you can't rightly say you have nothing by which to help extinguish fires within your church; God has given you the ability to act fearlessly and powerfully to make things happen (2 Timothy 1:7). Even if you're not among the primary individuals God is using to extinguish a fire within your church, you can nevertheless play a powerful part in helping those who are engrossed in the battle, as God leads you and instructs you how to "bear one another's burdens" (Galatians 6:2).

During the great fire, there were hundreds of individuals who could have easily joined the ranks of fellow Bostonians who had chosen to be bystanders, but they instead chose to spend their time and energy bearing some of the burdens of the firefighters. Because Boston, like most of the surrounding areas, was experiencing a horse-flu epizootic at the time, Boston's fire department had absolutely no healthy horses by which to pull fire engines and other heavy equipment to and from various locations. Firefighters had no choice but to manually pull their engines and haul their equipment on foot. That is until hundreds of individuals chose to step up and do the carting for them. These helpful citizens had never been trained in firefighting techniques, but they sure knew how to play-like-a-horse and get fire equipment where it needed to be. Not only did this help prevent firefighters from growing too exhausted to combat fires, it visually encouraged other would-be bystanders to search for ways they could be of help as well.

When a church fire is public and those fighting the fire are growing exhausted, you can likewise do your part to help others by alleviating some of the burdens. For instance, you can serve in areas of weakness, where a willing and faithful-hearted individual or group of individuals can make all the difference in the world! Such was the case when Moses was leading God's people in a physical battle against the warriors of Amalek (Exodus 17:8-13). God had tasked Moses with standing in a high place where he could be seen by Joshua and the other warriors of Israel, and Moses was to keep his hands (holding his staff) high in the air throughout the duration of the battle. Consequently,

73

whenever Moses' hands were down, the warriors of Amalek would gain ground in the battle, and whenever Moses' hands were up, those fighting with Joshua would advance against the enemy of God. As you can imagine, Moses grew rather exhausted doing his part in the gruesome firefight that God's people were facing. That is until others (Aaron and Hur) came to his aid and lent their strength where weakness had immerged. They gathered a stone for Moses to sit upon during the battle, and the two men held up Moses' hands until "Joshua overwhelmed Amalek and his people with the sword" (Exodus 17:13). Men who could have stood by only to watch the battle unfold, while Moses struggled to lead the fight, chose instead to do something! They chose to bear Moses' burdens by putting their strength where it was critically needed.

When your church is facing a fire and you're not one of the primary firefighters engaged in the fight, you can nevertheless lend your strength where it is critically needed. You can step up and temporarily serve in ways that may not require much skill and may not be how you've ever served before. (How much training was needed to pull fire engines around Boston or to hold up Moses' hands?) In fact, your strength can mean all the difference during a church fire, wherein filling in the gaps and helping the weak is what we're God-called to do (1 Thessalonians 5:14). At times, weaknesses that pop up within individuals will be other than physical, and we can serve one another's mental and spiritual conditions by way of encouraging one another and reminding one another of God's Word (1 Thessalonians 5:11, 2 Peter 1:12-15). Regardless of what the circumstances require, choose to serve others instead of idly doing nothing when fires rage within your church. Placing your strength where it's needed, especially when joining others in this endeavor, may be just the thing that births a positive turning point in your church's firefighting efforts.

Wet Blankets Can Save a Church

Another way you can help extinguish fires within your church is through prayer. While you may not be situated (positionally, physically, or otherwise) to help battle fires in other ways, prayer is always a very useful firefighting tool available to anyone who loves God and loves his church. Powerful things can happen when God's people pray (James 5:17-18). The Apostle Paul encouraged Christ followers to pray God's will on all occasions and to remain alert, in order to know when and how to pray for fellow Christ followers (Ephesians 6:18). In other words, when individuals alertly observe a public fire occurring within their church, all of them should immediately begin praying for those fighting against it – that God would strengthen them and direct them to do what's necessary to extinguish the fire.

Some call this practice "bathing a church in prayer," which is when individuals within a church collectively pray together to petition God to move mightily in helping to prevent and extinguish negative church fires. This *bathing* conveys a complete and prayerful covering of the church (from the pastors and staff to the lay leaders and the entire congregation), much like the covering of a human body when it is completely submerged in a bathtub of water. To bathe a church in prayer means that bystanders choose to stop doing *nothing* and instead begin to fervently pray for their church, as if its very survival depends upon their prayers – because it very well could!

During the great fire, a *bathing* of sorts took place that helped save the Old South Meeting House, which was a long-standing church wherein the Boston Tea Party revolt had organized nearly one hundred years earlier. After bystanders had watched many buildings (including several churches) burn to the ground, hundreds of them decided to give the Old South Meeting House a fighting chance for survival as the fire crept closer and closer to it. These bystanders stopped watching the fiery destruction of the great fire, and they went to work acquiring as many blankets as they could muster from nearby homes and businesses that had yet to be consumed by the fire. They then drenched the blankets with water, often from slow-dripping fountains (due to a lack of water pressure), and they went about covering the iconic church with wet blankets. As soon as they were successful at applying a great number of blankets to the church's roof, the fire began to encroach upon the parameters of the church. Men stationed themselves on the roof of the church to quickly stamp-out embers that fell on the church, as burning buildings directly adjacent to the church were spewing embers into the sky.

These former bystanders, who had literally bathed a church with wet blankets, were able to keep the Old South Meeting House protected long enough for firefighters to arrive and join the firefighting efforts.

While the great fire destroyed hundreds of buildings before it was eventually extinguished, the Old South Meeting House was not among those buildings! It remained standing, and still stands to this day, due in part because a host of former bystanders chose to form what some later called "the wet blanket brigade." This brigade of individuals had come to believe that working to save a church was a better choice than standing around and watching a church be destroyed.

Today, each church needs its own wet blanket brigade of prayerful individuals. Within that brigade should be every individual who loves God and wants to see him use the church for his purposes. There should be no bystanders in a church, as there is no excuse for any genuine Christ follower to stand by and do nothing while fires of negativity rage. While not everyone is positioned or appropriately equipped to fight a fire on the front lines of battle, everyone can nevertheless join the fight by bathing his church in prayer and petitioning God to do the miraculous!

When each individual within a church is praying for his church and expecting God to move mightily, God's glory is made known to more people when he sovereignly acts in powerful ways. Additionally, when each individual within a church is communicating with God about church fires, then each individual is better positioned to receive instructions from God regarding how he may do *more* than pray; there may be embers that God directs some individuals to quickly stomp-out! A church's wet blanket brigade is not about ganging up on God and forcing him to do something about church fires; that's not how God operates. Rather, the more individuals who are praying about a public fire means a greater number of people are preparing themselves to see God's glory manifested and possibly to receive firefighting instructions from God. For these reasons, *everyone* should be in the wet blanket brigade!

Get to Work or Get Out of the Way!

Bystanders inhibit others from fighting fires, and there's no room for individuals like these on the battle lines of any of God's churches. Therefore, if you're not going to help fight fires within your church, you need to step aside and stay out of the way of those who are fighting – at least until you decide to join your fellow Christ followers in the battle. When Jesus was fighting the ultimate fires of sin and death, he once told the Apostle Peter to get out of his way (Matthew 16:21-23). On this occasion, Peter had become a bystander who had chosen to *supervise* Jesus by telling him that his firefighting tactics (regarding suffering, dying, and being raised again to defeat sin) were entirely the wrong way to go. Jesus then told Peter to get behind him and likened Peter's actions to the work of Satan. Jesus went on to call Peter a hindrance to his firefighting mission.

Individuals who are determined to do nothing productive during church-threatening fires should heed the very words that Jesus spoke to Peter on that specific occasion; they should remove themselves from the scene of the battle so that others can go about firefighting without being hindered. To stick around gawking, supervising, and slowing down God's work is to elicit even more destruction within a church. Therefore, either get to work helping your church fight fires, or get out of the way! You have no business dabbling and nosing into the affairs of a church within which you're not properly invested, especially if lending your strength in areas of weakness and fervently praying for your church are not on your agenda.

For those of you willing to serve your church during the heat of battle, know that your church desperately needs you. When negative fires are threatening your church, you can help extinguish them by bearing the burdens of others and lending your strength in areas of weakness. You can fervently pray for your church, witness God's glory, and often receive firefighting instructions to carry out. In doing these things, you'll keep yourself from becoming a bystander. In serving your church during some of its most trying circumstances, you'll play a critical role in helping to extinguish fires and helping to safeguard the work of God within your church.

8

Fighting Fire with Fire Backfired
Deal with Bullies and Others Without
Adopting Bully Tactics

As Bostonians watched the great fire destroy their city, the realization that the fire was not going to be easily or timely contained began to dominate their thinking. It became very apparent to Bostonians that their city had been ill-prepared to effectively fight a fire of this magnitude, and many Bostonians naturally began to entertain the idea of using an extreme measure to fight the ever-growing fire. That measure entailed using tons of gunpowder to blow up homes and businesses within the fire's path to keep the fire from moving past the purposefully-demolished buildings.

Boston's Fire Chief John Damrell was entirely against the idea of "fighting fire with fire" to combat the great fire within his city. Moreover, according to Boston's regulations, Damrell was the only person who could order that such a tactic be employed. Not even the mayor, nor anyone else in Boston, had the authority to supersede Damrell's decision on the matter. Therefore, after the great fire had been growing for many hours, many of those who were eager to use gunpowder began to collectively bully Damrell into making the decision to blow up buildings within Boston. The mayor and other city officials repeatedly summoned Damrell to several emergency meetings throughout the night (which Damrell was required to attend, even though it meant he had to temporarily leave the line of duty amidst the biggest firefight of his life). At these meetings, city officials shouted at Damrell and called him names, and they told him that if he didn't order the demolition of buildings, he *alone* would be responsible for allowing the great fire to destroy the entire city.

It wasn't until city officials began to circulate the rumor that Boston's Fire Chief had literally gone insane under the pressures of fighting the great fire that Damrell appeared at a final emergency meeting to emphatically declare his sanity and to reluctantly acquiesce to the demands that gunpowder be used to fight the great fire. He gave the orders to secure gunpowder from various locations and to begin blowing up a host of buildings that were determined to be in the path of the fire.

Unfortunately, the tactic not only proved insufficient at stopping or slowing the great fire, but it made matters worse. Gunpowder was brought in by the tons from the Navy Yard, other federal depositories, and the powder boat in the Boston Harbor. Even more gunpowder was collected from trains that came into Boston. Dozens of buildings were then blown to smithereens, and Bostonians later watched the great fire merely leap right over those destroyed buildings and carry on just as forcibly as before. In fact, the explosions only aided the great fire in some respects, as additional gas lines were damaged and new fires began. Sometimes flying debris from the gunpowder-induced explosions would damage surrounding buildings, knocking out windows and creating holes within the outside walls of the buildings. This allowed fires to easily and quickly enter some of those buildings and begin burning them down.

Boston's last-ditch endeavor to fight fire with fire had backfired. After many homes and businesses had been purposefully destroyed by gunpowder, and having nothing positive to show for it, Damrell ordered that no further buildings should be blown up. It wasn't for several hours later (about 12 hours after the great fire had first begun) that the fire finally came to an end.

Fighting Fire with Fire Always Backfires in a Church

When fires of negativity aren't properly prevented or extinguished within churches, many individuals resort to fighting fire with fire. In other words, these individuals toss to the wind all biblical instruction and guidance from the Holy Spirit, and they become renegades who take matters into their own hands. For example, they engage in nefarious power struggles, they lash out at others, they seek to take revenge on others, they gossip about others, and they do more still.

Sometimes, fighting fire with fire happens when church members (some of whom may want nothing but the best for their church) get caught up in behaving in the same sinful and destructive manners as those who are responsible for starting or propagating church fires. And the result is always the same: fires of negativity within a church only grow and cause more pain and damage when they're combated with more negativity. Arguments seem to never end, more people leave the church, real ministry is sometimes brought to a stand-still, and Satan sits back and watches the fire-on-fire calamity with a huge grin on his wicked face.

Nevertheless, God's Word is replete with warnings against fighting fire with fire. It makes it rather clear that such tactics are never appropriate. The Apostle Paul wrote to all Christ followers, "Repay no one evil for evil, but give thought to do what is honorable in the sight of all. If possible, so far as it depends on you, live peaceably with all. Beloved, never avenge yourselves, but leave it to the wrath of God, for it is written, 'Vengeance is mine, I will repay, says the Lord '" (Romans 12:17-19). In other words, there's never an appropriate circumstance in which to allow sinful and negative attitudes and actions to be deployed toward others. Each of us should strive to combat negativity through honorable and peaceable means, and we should always allow God (without any help from us) to punish those who instigate negativity and desire to see it thrive.

Because fighting fire with fire should never be employed, Paul instructed overseers and elders (pastors) to be "self-controlled, not violent but gentle, not quarrelsome, and not quick-tempered" (1 Timothy 3:2-3, Titus 1:7-8). Pastors and elders are to set a proper example for the rest of the church family (1 Peter 5:3). When someone in a leadership position begins fighting fires with fire, it's not long before others within the church are doing the same thing. Pastors, more than others, should know better than to engage in fire-on-fire combat, and they should be more adept at conforming to the biblical standards of firefighting that are honorable and peace-seeking.

Acting Honorably and Peaceably is Not the Same as Being Passive

Fighting fires honorably and peaceably doesn't mean that firm and decisive actions are not in order. Correcting and rebuking others is a biblical requirement. Sometimes those who behave very negatively must be dealt with in very uncomfortable ways (1 Corinthians 5:1-13), but in strength and with confidence that comes from following God's Word. Also, for fires of negativity to be properly addressed, we are to speak the truth in love (Ephesians 4:15), and God's Word, rather than our own opinions and desires, should always be dictating our words and actions (Colossians 3:16-17). Moreover, a desire for restoration and an attitude of gentleness should always be our modus operandi toward anyone observed to be behaving in negative and sinful ways (Galatians 6:1). And finally, our firefighting should always be done carefully, so that we might not engage within additional fires of negativity of our own making (Galatians 6:2).

When it comes to preventing and extinguishing fires of negativity within our churches, we should always strive to do so in a manner that holds-fast to our high calling as Christ followers. May each of us learn to follow the words of instruction that Paul gave to the Colossian church: "Put on then, as God's chosen ones, holy and beloved, compassionate hearts, kindness, humility, meekness, and patience, bearing with one another and, if one has a complaint against another, forgiving each other; as the Lord has forgiven you, so you also must forgive. And above all these put on love, which binds everything together in perfect harmony. And let the peace of Christ rule in your hearts, to which indeed you were called in one body" (Colossians 3:12-15). Our high calling as Christ followers leaves absolutely no room for combating fire with fire.

Bullies Love Fireworks

Because Fire Chief Damrell was initially so adamant against the use of gunpowder, city officials and other Bostonians tried their best to bully him into submitting to their will. They wanted things done *their* way, and they didn't care what they had to do to ensure that gunpowder would be used to demolish buildings. In fact, many Bostonians, especially former Civil War General Henry W. Benham, seemed to be itching to blow up as many buildings as possible. It's like the great fire had produced an opportunity to do what was very uncommon, and some individuals seemed to revel at the chance to blow things up. Therefore, the name calling, the pressures of mandatory meetings during the heat of battle, and the spreading of vicious rumors regarding Damrell's sanity were continued. All of these things ultimately persuaded Damrell to give-in and surrender to the bullies exactly what they wanted, which resulted in more destruction upon the city.

Hours later, after Damrell had witnessed the devasting effects of the gunpower and could not bear to see it last any longer, Damrell decided to reverse his decision and put an end to the manmade demolitions. It was a challenge to get some individuals to comply. Once General Benham and others had been let-loose to do what should never have been allowed in the first place, they weren't all too willing to cease and desist just because a higher authority demanded it. Bullies don't like to be reigned-in and forced to behave in manners that are against their wishes, especially after they've been previously successful at bullying others and getting what they want. Therefore, Damrell ultimately had to send hand-written orders, which included promises of arrest for non-compliance, in the hands of fire captains and others to those who were carrying out the demolitions, and the demolitions stopped soon after. Even General Benham begrudgingly chose to comply after realizing the consequences he would face if he ignored the order.

Sadly, bullies exist within churches, too. They're often responsible for starting and fueling fires of negativity, and like General Benham, they're often itching for fireworks (verbal fights and power wars) and willing do whatever it takes to get their way. Church bullies don't care about who they railroad or what they might have to do to dominate and manipulate others; their only objective is getting their way at all costs – no matter how much fiery damage is caused in the process or the aftermath. Nevertheless, we must be willing to stand our ground, face church bullies head on, and deal with them appropriately before their bully tactics result in further damage to the churches that we call family.

How to Defeat Bullies Without Using Bully Tactics

We're very fortunate that the Apostle John provided crucial information concerning how to appropriately deal with church bullies (without forgoing the mandate to act honorably and peaceably), as he described his own interaction with a church bully. He wrote, "I have written something to the church, but Diotrephes, who likes to put himself first, does not acknowledge our authority. So if I come, I will bring up what he is doing, talking wicked nonsense against us. And not content with that, he refuses to welcome the brothers, and also stops those who want to and puts them out of the church" (3 John 1:9-10).

The bully with whom John dealt was very similar to the church bullies that exist in today's churches. They put themselves first, they abhor authority, they spread slanderous things about those in opposition to them, and they try to dominate and ostracize anyone who disagrees with them. Unsurprisingly then, today's church bullies must be firmly opposed in the same ways (below) that John stood up to Diotrephes:

- John publicly denounced the bully tactics of Diotrephes, and he called him out by name. Bullies can hardly be rebuffed privately without more problems ensuing, as bullies typically have an audience that is aware of what they've been doing. That audience (whether it is a small group of people or an entire church) needs to witness a bully's reprimand. John wrote a letter that he knew would be passed around and publicly read, and he used the very name of the bully he was chastising in his letter. He didn't want to be too general in his verbiage. It was necessary that he be very specific, as bullies must be personally and publicly called on the carpet and held accountable for their actions.

- Secondly, John proceeded to list the undignified offenses of Diotrephes. He didn't write, "Diotrephes is a bully in need of correction, and you're going to have to take my word for it." Instead, he carefully itemized each ungodly behavior of which Diotrephes was guilty. He exposed the bully tactics for what they were. John wanted the church to understand exactly how Diotrephes had erred, and he couldn't afford to be discreet. Bully situations rarely call for discretion, as public and powerful bullies will try to trounce and overpower those who passively attempt to combat them behind closed doors.

- Thirdly, John included in his letter his willingness to continue the process of correction with Diotrephes. He said that he was going to "bring up" the matter yet again, albeit in person, if the opportunity availed itself. John understood that bullies are often hard-headed recidivists, and they typically need to be perpetually rebuffed. If John's public letter had not propelled others within Diotrephes' church to stand up to him (as it likely did), John was ready to personally bear the burden even further, if it was needed. He was willing to stand up to Diotrephes for as long as it took, because he didn't want to see bully-induced fires spreading and stifling ministry any further.

When we respond to bullies in the way that John responded to Diotrephes, we can appropriately put bullies in their place without stepping outside the parameters of honorable and peaceable living. For that matter, there's simply no reason we should ever put ourselves above others (Philippians 2:3), disrespect spiritual authority (1 Thessalonians 5:12), slander others (1 Peter 2:1), gossip about others (2 Corinthians 12:20), seek to dominate others (Matthew 20:26), or try to excommunicate those who may not agree with our opinions, ideas, and preferences (Ephesians 4:2). Instead, by publicly denouncing bullies by name, by publicly identifying their wicked behaviors, and by constantly standing up to them and holding their feet to the fire, we can defeat bullies, and their fiery activities can be extinguished.

Moreover, when many church members rally together to correct individual bullies or groups of bullies within their church, the fire extinguishing can sometimes occur more swiftly. There's power in numbers, and the biggest of bullies often quickly cower and submit to righteous rebuke when they realize that they're up against a large group of selfless, God-focused Christ followers who are determined to band together and carry the torch against them. When church members collectively endeavor to behave honorably, strive to live peaceably, and act boldly and appropriately toward the threats of bullies, churches are strengthened and made more invincible to fiery calamities.

9

History Doesn't Have to Repeat Itself
Selflessly Love One Another

The great fire that had snuck up on Boston one Saturday evening and destroyed most of its financial district finally came to an end the following morning. After raging for more than 12 hours, it ended only a couple of hours before many Bostonians were to meet for Sunday worship services within church buildings scattered throughout the city. Despite the grim circumstances, most churches kept to their schedules and conducted services. Church buildings that had been destroyed or severely damaged didn't necessitate canceled meetings, as congregations were directed to alternate meeting places which included public squares and music halls.

Church services were packed. They were filled to standing-room only, and some churches even chose to conduct additional services throughout the day, as thousands of people were turned away from earlier services. Even though the greater percentage of Bostonians had spent the entire night awake with the fire, it didn't stop many of them from convening with their congregations that Sunday to see and encourage one another, to pray together, and to receive hope and instruction from God's Word during their most desperate and trying of circumstances.

Most pastors had scrapped their previously planned sermons and had crafted new messages around the fiery tragedy that had just occurred. During the service at the Somerset-street Baptist Church, for instance, the Reverend John F. Beckley opened his message by reminding listeners that everyone's life-work will be revealed and tested by fire to see what has been built on the foundation of Christ (1 Corinthians 3:10-14). Using the great fire as an object lesson of sorts, he stressed that *selfishness* was not in line with proper building procedures, as it always receives divine rebuke. He then alluded to Boston's unwillingness to widen dangerously narrow roads, its building of large warehouses with eye-pleasing mansard roofs (which were always known to be fire-fuelers), and its blatant disregard of fire-preventative measures and warnings, like those Fire Chief Damrell had given. Beckley charged Boston with being guilty of its own destruction, as its selfishness was unrestrained. He then admonished his listeners to selflessly build their lives (and rebuild their city) in a way that could stand the test of fire.

Reverend Beckley concluded his message by begging his listeners (and all of Boston, for that matter) to have a deeper love for one another, to compassionately consider how various actions might endanger one another, and to be committed to the wellbeing of everyone as a whole – rather than everyone merely being concerned with himself. Beckley asserted that these three pleas were in fact God's message and desire for Boston in the wake of the great fire. Selfishness could no longer rule the day without the penalty of a debilitating fire arising as a consequence. It needed to be annihilated going forward, and brotherly love is what needed to take its place.

Selfishness is the Cause of Many Church Fires

Reverend Beckley's message holds true today; selfishness simply cannot be permitted within churches that are striving to fulfill their God-ordained missions. It merely provides Satan with an abundance of opportunities to begin monstrous church fires. And then he takes those fires and uses them to easily and methodically dismantle churches piece by piece. When Christ followers are consumed with protecting and advancing their own individual desires and preferences at all costs, their selfish behaviors sow fiery seeds that always sprout and come to fruition in the worst possible ways. Just as Beckley told his congregation so many years ago, today's congregations must have love, compassion, and commitment (toward the welfare of the entire church family) deeply rooted within the hearts of its members.

The Apostle Paul shared a similar message to the church at Philippi many years before Reverend Beckley spoke before his own congregation. Paul wrote, "So if there is any encouragement in Christ, any comfort from love, any participation in the Spirit, any affection and sympathy, complete my joy by being of the same mind, having the same love, being in full accord and of one mind. Do nothing from selfish ambition or conceit, but in humility count others more significant than yourselves. Let each of you look not only to his own interests, but also to the interests of others" (Philippians 2:1-4). Paul didn't want to see the Philippian church (or any other church of God) consumed with fires set ablaze by selfishness, so he stressed the importance of members compassionately loving one another in a way that would promote the welfare of the entire church body. He wasn't telling the Philippians that they couldn't have preferences and interests different from those of others; he was merely explaining that those preferences and interests should never be pitted against one another in a battle. In other words, each member of a church family should selflessly come together in "full accord and of one mind" amid differences, and their preeminent focus should be on unity and group health as their plans and decisions are fleshed out.

Sadly, however, some church families fail to heed Paul's instructions. Individuals and groups within these churches are always fighting to advance personal preferences and ideas. In these church families (which might better be described as war zones), members view those in agreement with them as fellow soldiers fighting for the cause, while anyone who disagrees with them is their enemy. Churches are divided into sides, and members will do whatever it takes to see that *their* side prevails while their opposition is soundly defeated. Campaigns are waged, power plays occur, bickering and complaining against one another ensues, and members fight it out to the bitter end. But that's the thing; there's rarely an *end* to the fighting. And yet, there's a lot of *bitter* that carries on, as warring church members typically find one thing after another to fight about. Many of those things can even be very petty, but a church with *fighting* in its DNA has never seen something too small or inconsequential over which squabbling and quarreling could not masterfully be done. And while they fight, Satan gleefully and carefully pushes and prods warring members (like logs within a bonfire) to keep church fires blazing.

When church members are strictly consumed with themselves, church families no longer operate as God intended – as *families*. There is division instead of unity, and fires of negativity rage. But when church members are endeavoring to do nothing out of selfishness, but they are humbly counting others more significant than themselves (Philippians 2:3), unity and family become a churches DNA, and fires are thwarted and minimized. Only when church members are selflessly loving one another can they behave in ways that promote the church family instead of individuals and groups. Selfless love is what allows church families to remain in "full accord and one mind" (Philippians 2:2), even as individuals and groups face preferential setbacks.

Selfless Love is Our Calling

The Reverend James Freeman Clarke of The Church of the Disciples spoke to a packed house in the aftermath of the great fire. His Sunday message included the account of an elderly, poor man who had been seen forsaking his own home (worth only $100) to save a woman from a burning building nearby. The man's house and all of his belongings were destroyed by the great fire, but the man wasn't the least bit regretful about what he had chosen to do. When later asked about why he had stopped fighting to protect what was his, he simply explained that it was his obligation instead to step in and save the woman, even if God allowed his own house to be destroyed in the process. "If it is God's will, it ought to be my pleasure! And it shall be!" the man emphatically said.

All Christ followers would do well to emulate the attitude and behavior of this inspiring man. We are to selflessly prefer and protect others, even when doing so requires us to first stop fighting to protect what is ours. Paul wrote, "We who are strong have an obligation to bear with the failings of the weak, and not to please ourselves. Let each of us please his neighbor for his good, to build him up" (Romans 15:1-2). Paul called it an *obligation*. In other words, it's part of our calling as Christ followers to promote others, even when doing so requires personal sacrifices. Paul went on to write that Jesus (our utmost example), "did not please himself," but he sacrificially took upon himself the burdens of others (Romans 15:3). May each of us be willing to do likewise as we follow Christ's lead.

When we're selflessly serving and promoting others, even when it requires us to forsake our own rights and desires in the process, God does amazing things within our churches. Fires of negativity are prevented and extinguished, unity within our church families is strengthened, and our churches move forward in a strong and healthy manner. All the while, our own uncomfortable circumstances don't have to get the best of us when we don't get our way as individuals, because we can respond to any setbacks that may befall us by trusting in God's sovereignty and remembering that our truest pleasure is living unto him. Like the poor man who chose to serve another over protecting what was his, each of us can say about our personal losses, "If it's God's will, it ought to be my pleasure! And it shall be!"

Endeavor to let that selfless sentiment become your mantra when things don't go your way. For instance, when your church stays together and thrives, but your musical preferences take a hit, let God know that you're nevertheless pleased to be in his service within your growing and healthy church. When your church is trying new things and reaching new people, but some of the traditions you've always fancied no longer carry the clout they once did, be so overjoyed about the progress that your church is making (and the lives that are being changed) that it dwarfs any grief you may experience regarding your dearly missed traditions. When programs, plans, and pastors aren't exactly what you desire them to be, be abundantly more thankful and pleased that indeed your church *has* programs, plans, and pastors than you are disappointed over the fact that your personal wish-list isn't being realized within all situations. Simply put, let your love, care, and commitment to the wellbeing of your church as a whole preempt any selfish tendencies to make *your* preferences predominant. And when things don't go your way, praise God anyway!

Conversely, if you and others are more eager to go about fighting to protect and advance your own personal agendas and wish-lists than remaining unified and healthy under the Lordship of Christ, then your church will pay a royal price. *Fighting* will be your church's favorite pastime, how it is known by outsiders, and what ultimately begets and grows one fire after another – until perhaps your church is permanently destroyed. Paul wrote to the Galatians, "For the whole law is fulfilled in one word: 'You shall love your neighbor as yourself.' But if you bite and devour one another, watch out that you are not consumed by one another (Galatians 5:14-15). Without selfless love for one another, church members will ultimately be responsible for their own demise as a church family. Therefore, may we all choose to lay aside selfish attitudes and desires and embrace what matters most: selfless love for our brothers and sisters in Christ. Our calling requires it, and our churches are depending on it to stay alive and fruitful!

It's Time to Get to Work

Are you ready to see Reverend Beckley's message realized within your church? If members of your church are striving to increase their love, care, and commitment toward one another, selfishness won't be the catalyst Satan can use for inflicting maximum damage, and you and others can selflessly go about preventing and extinguishing fires.

On *that* note, start putting to practice what you've learned in this book, if you haven't done so already. Ask God to help you and every member of your church to rise to the occasion and fight fires in these ways:

- Step up and start serving where your talents are best used, even when doing so makes you susceptible to underappreciation and abuse.

- Always seek God's guidance regarding the best time and manner to do things, including blessing others and fighting fires.

- Fight fires with an abundance of fresh power from God, as you know and belong to Christ, live righteously, and endeavor to be more about living in power than talking about power.

- Know and follow God's Word, and strive to make God's Word preeminent within your life and the life of your church on all occasions.

- Never try to personally gain from a fire of negativity within your church, but always do whatever you can do to extinguish fires and minimize damage.

- Never sit by and watch a fire of negativity destroy your church, but lend your aid whenever possible, pray fervently for your church, and do whatever God specifically directs you to do to prevent and extinguish fires.

- Fight fires honorably and peaceably, and deal with bullies appropriately, while never employing bully tactics of your own.

- And finally, selflessly love and protect your church family, as unity and church health (being in full accord and of one mind) is always at the forefront.

When you and others within your church begin to employ these tactics faithfully, your church's chances of succumbing to the damage or the ruinous demise of a Boston fire of negativity will be greatly diminished. When it comes to Boston fires, history doesn't have to figuratively repeat itself within your church, and it's up to you and your church to ensure that it doesn't. So, get to work and start fireproofing your church in all the right ways!

Selected Bibliography

Boston Historic Society. A Walk Through the City's Fire
and Firefighting History: Boston's Fire Trail.
Charleston: The History Press, 2007.

Coffin, Charles Carleton, An Eye-witness. *The Story of
The Great Fire, Boston, November 9-10, 1872*.
Boston: Shepard and Gill, 1872

Conwell, Col. R. H. *History of the Great Fire in Boston*.
Boston: B. B. Russell, 1872.

Damrell's Fire. (2005). [DVD] Directed by B. Twickler.
Docema, LLC & WSBE/Rhode Island PBS.

Murdock, Harold. *Letters Written by a Gentleman in
Boston to his Friend in Paris Describing the Great
Fire*. Boston: Houghton Mifflin Company, 1873.

Report of the Commissioners Appointed to Investigate the Cause and Management. Boston: Rockwell & Churchhill, City Printers, 1873.

Sammarco, Anthony Mitchell. *Images of America: The Boston Fire of 1872.* Charleston: Arcadia Publishing, 1997.

Schorow, Stephanue. *Boston On Fire.* Beverly: Commonwealth Editions, 2003.

A large portion of the stories regarding the interesting behaviors of various individuals during and after the great fire were learned from Conwell's *History of the Great Fire in Boston.* Conwell witnessed many of the events firsthand, and he also recorded eyewitness accounts from many others as well. Conwell's book, written in the weeks just after the great fire, was an invaluable resource in the writing of this book.

"Euchred, Pard!"

The Advantage is Yours, in Christ

In the days immediately following the great fire, barriers were erected and stationed with soldiers around the burnt district of Boston to keep people from rummaging around. This was done to prevent theft, but the blockade was also necessary to prevent onlookers from getting in the way of officials to whom access had been granted. Thousands of Bostonians, along with thousands of others from outside of Boston, had flooded the area merely to get an eye-full of the devastation, and these sightseers had to be restricted from critical areas. Typically, before someone could gain access through a barrier, he first had to have a pass given to him by either Fire Chief Damrell, E. H. Savage (the Chief of Police), or by a general commanding the troops that were stationed at the barriers. Without such a pass, individuals were not permitted to pass through the blockade, regardless of the varying tactics that some of them used in their attempts to skirt protocol.

For example, one man tried to use intimidation to

garner his way through the barricade. Upon attempting to enter a restricted area, a young soldier (possibly only a teenager) sternly informed him that he would be denied passage. Outraged, the man began to belittle the young soldier for presuming to be so bold toward his elder, and he mockingly said to him, "Say sonny, who did you do whitewashing for before your mother bought you that soldier coat?" Undeterred, the young soldier stood his ground, and the older man soon realized that his intimidation tactics would not win him access through the barrier.

Another individual who was well dressed and who apparently considered himself very important tried to pass the barrier, and like everyone else without a pass, he was denied. He arrogantly argued with the soldiers and informed them that they had no right to prevent someone of his stature from passing. The man's attitude screamed, "Don't you know who I am?!" One of the soldiers was quick to inform him, "You cannot pass here without an order, even if you are the president of the United States!" After arguing a little longer, the proud individual finally turned around and walked away in defeat. He took his bruised ego with him.

Countless others were denied access through the barriers, even as they tried to explain their good intentions. Some referenced the good things they had done to merit access, such as their previous involvement in the fire fight. Nevertheless, many were surprised to learn that their good deeds weren't sufficient for gaining access.

And yet, not everyone was denied access through

the blockade, of course. There were those to whom passes had been granted for various reasons, and these individuals sometimes took great pleasure in presenting their passes to unsuspecting troops who were all too eager and ready to force them to turn around and leave. For example, one individual approached the barrier and received the typical salutation from one of the soldiers: "You cannot pass here!" Instead of arguing with the soldiers, the man simply reached into his pocket, fetched a hand-written note from the chief of police, and handed it to one of the soldiers. He then curtly walked through the checkpoint and said to the soldier to whom he had given the note, "I guess I'll not only pass, but go it alone." He then winked at another nearby soldier and said, "Euchred, pard!" as he entered the burnt district without any obstruction.

The man's parting terminology had come from a game called Euchre, which was a very popular game at the time. When he mentioned going through the barrier "alone," it's because a player on a two-person team in Euchre could ultimately win the game without his teammate winning along with him. And the expression, "Euchred, pard" was a way of announcing, "I've got the advantage (or I've won), my friend!" This Euchre-playing man no doubt reveled over his hand-written pass, and he wasn't the least bit apprehensive to let others know it. And yet, it was the *pass* which had been provided to him in the name and authority of another that granted him access through the blockade. Absolutely *nothing* regarding the man's own wherewithal permitted him access. In other words, if the prospect of entering had been solely up to him, he would have been turned away like many others. Only what had been given to him by the power and signature of an official did the trick!

We, Too, Face a Barrier

In the same way that barriers had been placed around the burnt district of Boston, the sinful disposition of humankind has placed a barrier between all people and God. Every person, based solely upon his own merits, is prevented from entering God's holy (sinless) presence and remaining with him for an eternity.

> **Romans 3:10-12**
> **10 "None is righteous, no, not one;**
> **11 no one understands;**
> **no one seeks for God.**
> **12 All have turned aside; together they have become worthless;**
> **no one does good,**
> **not even one."**

> **Romans 3:23**
> **23 For all have sinned and fall short of the glory of God.**

> **Romans 6:23(a)**
> **23 For the wages of sin is death.**

Each of us have sinned; we've gone our own way and done things of which God doesn't approve. The penalty of those sins is spiritual death, which includes an ugly and miserable existence far from God, both here on earth and into the afterlife (after we physically perish). There is nothing that we can do to remedy this situation.

Try as we might to pass through the barrier of our sin and into God's presence, we'll always fail. We can't intimidate-our-way into God's graces, our claims of self-importance will never suffice, and we can't even hang our hats on the list of seemingly good things we've done to tip the scales in our favor and allow us to proceed past our sins and into God's lasting embrace. Simply put, none of us can overcome our sin, and we all deserve to be apart from God forever.

There is a Pass

But there's good news! Like the hand-written passes that were given by officials to allow access through the barriers in Boston, there is a pass that can grant individuals access through the barrier of their sin and into the presence of their creator for an eternity. That pass comes from Jesus Christ, the one and only official through whom God has made these divine passes available.

Romans 6:23
[23] For the wages of sin is death, but the free gift of God is eternal life in Christ Jesus our Lord.

Romans 5:6-8
[6] For while we were still weak, at the right time Christ died for the ungodly. [7] For one will scarcely die for a righteous person—though perhaps for a good person one would dare even to die— [8] but God shows his love for us in that while we were still

sinners, Christ died for us.

A divine pass (or free gift) was created when the innocent son of God, Jesus Christ, died on the cross and received in himself the punishment for sin. The pass is powerful and authoritative. It's not hand-written, but it's blood-written. And when individuals receive the pass provided by Jesus Christ, they are granted access into an eternal relationship with the risen Savior and his Father. Sin ceases to be a barrier, and the unparalleled advantage belongs to the pass holder – in the name of Jesus Christ!

Passes are always singular and applicable to the individual possessing it. Like the Euchre-playing man who said, "I'll go it alone," each of us must possess our own pass from Jesus Christ and thus pass the barrier of our sins unaccompanied by others. In other words, others cannot rely on us and we cannot rely on the passes of others to grant us access to God. If our family members or friends know Christ and possess blood-written passes, we will not be granted access to God simply because of our relationships with them. We must each possess our own pass, and we must each "go it alone" when passing through the barrier of our sins and entering into the eternal life made possible through Jesus Christ.

Are You a Pass Holder?

If you're a pass holder, you know what it's like to be a "new creation" (2 Corinthians 5:17), having passed through the barrier of your sin and now living for Christ and belonging to him forever. Hopefully, you're perpetually growing in your relationship with Jesus, you're walking in light of his Word instead of living like someone without a blood-written pass (how you once lived), and you're helping to fight fires with the power that God's Holy Spirit provides.

If you're not a pass holder, perhaps today is the day that will change! While there's nothing you can do to overcome the sin barrier that exists between you and God, you might take hold of God's free gift of salvation by laying your sinful life at God's feet and acknowledging unto him that you're in desperate need of a divine pass through his son Jesus Christ. If God's Holy Spirit is drawing you toward him even now, won't you cry out to him and trade your life of sin for his divine pass?

> **Romans 10:9-10**
> **⁹ If you confess with your mouth that Jesus is Lord and believe in your heart that God raised him from the dead, you will be saved.¹⁰ For with the heart one believes and is justified, and with the mouth one confesses and is saved.**

> **Romans 10:13**
> **¹³ For "everyone who calls on the name of the Lord will be saved."**

Everyone who genuinely calls on the name of Jesus (the pass-distributor) will be given a pass. He will be forgiven of his sins, made new in Christ, and empowered to fight fires of negativity along with his fellow Christ followers. Speaking of which, if you've just become a new pass holder yourself, make sure to find and join a Bible-believing church as soon as possible. Just because you entered your new life in Christ *alone* (with your own pass) doesn't mean God wants you to live for him without being in the company of other pass holders who belong to him as well. On the contrary, Christ followers are to meet together regularly and serve one another in a number of ways (Hebrews 10:25). Moreover, there are so many things waiting to be learned and experienced by new Christ followers, and you need a local expression of God's family to help you along the way.

Therefore, connect with a church, and don't hesitate to let other pass holders know about your own newly acquired pass. For that matter, let *everyone* know what Jesus Christ has done for you, including those who currently don't have passes. Perhaps some may hear your testimony, confess Jesus, and acquire passes of their own, so don't let anything stop you from sharing with others how you were enabled (and by whom) to pass through the barrier of your sin. You can even say to them, "I've got the advantage, friend!" when you're describing your new life in Christ, but you probably don't want to smugly *wink* at them in the process. Ha!

Small Group Study Guide
Nine Sessions

How It Works

These nine sessions are designed to be used in a small[1] group setting wherein discussion is welcomed and encouraged, and they correspond with the nine chapters of the book. Each session's material should take approximately 35 to 45 minutes[2] to read and discuss within a talkative group, and all participants are expected to have read the chapter corresponding to a session before that session begins. For example, the first session will cover the first chapter, so make sure that group members receive their books and know to read at least the first chapter before the first session.

Group members are encouraged to bring their books to each session. A group leader should be prepared to read aloud each session's material and to facilitate discussion among members of the group during the meetings. All members are encouraged to follow the session material from their own books as the group leader reads aloud. Leaders should be prepared to share their own insights and responses for each of the items within each session, especially if others within the group are initially hesitant to contribute to the discussion. Keep in mind that some individuals will need a little time to grow comfortable with the group before they are willing to speak in a group setting, while other individuals may never feel compelled to share. Both situations are normal, and no one should ever be forced to share or made to feel uncomfortable for not sharing.

If you have other items (such as personal prayer needs, church announcements, and other things) that will take place within your small group sessions, they can be done before or after your group covers the material within this guide. These sessions should be compatible with pre-existing church group meetings of all kinds, from Sunday school groups to cell groups that meet at various times.

[1] The ideal number of participants for a small group will vary from church to church, but a key ingredient of these sessions is the discussion that should take place within the group. This material will best be used in groups wherein members are encouraged to share and learn together, and larger groups wherein discussion is not permitted do not afford that experience. Perhaps teachers and pastors could incorporate the material into lectures or sermons, but this may not prove as successful at undergirding the principles outlined within this book as would the intimate discussion that is allowed within small groups.

[2] The first session may run slightly shorter than the others.

Suggestions for Group Study Sessions

The following suggestions are not necessary to host successful and productive sessions, but they could prove helpful in getting the attention of your group members, fostering excitement about the nine-week course, and strengthening commitment from the group members to do the required reading before each session. Please do whatever is most beneficial for your group, as all groups are different.

Room Décor: You may want to acquire fire related props from a party story or Amazon.com and place a few within your meeting space. Large cardboard cutouts of fire flames can be placed on the floor and smaller cutouts can be placed on tables (if your group uses tables) as centerpieces. If your budget is limited and you have creative individuals within your group, perhaps props can be made instead of purchased.

Audio: If you have a sound system available, you may want to have the sound of a crackling fire playing while group members are arriving and fellowshipping before the session begins. If you have a television or projector system available, you could incorporate a video (fire flames) that loops continuously until you stop the presentation. You can purchase and download audio and video files, or you can find them on YouTube.com.

Food: If your group meetings typically entail snack foods, you could incorporate fire themed paper products (napkins, cups, plates) and foods, such as cupcakes with icing that looks like fire. These products can be purchased from a party store or Amazon.com, or (regarding various food items) they can be made by members of your group.

Extras: If your budget allows, you could order fire related novelty items (from orientaltrading.com or one of several imprint novelty sites). Fire hydrant magnets or similar items could be given to group members before or during the first session to remind them to keep up with their readings each week.

Room Temperature: If you can pull it off, make the room wherein your group will meet as swelteringly hot as possible, in keeping with the whole fire themed endeavor. Just kidding! – Instead, be sure to keep the room temperature comfortable so your group members can better focus on the material within each session.

The Great Boston Fire of 1872
Your Church Could Face Its Own Boston Fire

*This session corresponds with Chapter One,
which begins on page 1.*

How to Begin:

Open the session with prayer. Ask God to allow the discussion to be encouraging and beneficial.

Ice-Breaker Questions:

1. What grabbed your attention the most in this chapter? In other words, what opened your eyes and led you to think about things you may not have thought about before?

2. Was there a biblical passage discussed in this chapter that really stepped on your toes?

Other Questions:

3. Read Ephesians 6:10-18 (below).

   a. Whose responsibility is it to extinguish the flaming darts of Satan?

   b. Did the Apostle Paul believe standing "against the schemes of the devil" to be important? How many times did he reference *standing?*

   c. Are there any circumstances wherein we're *not* to be ready to extinguish satanic fires (verse 16)?

Ephesians 6:10-18
[10] Finally, be strong in the Lord and in the strength of his might. [11] Put on the whole armor of God, that you may be able to stand against the schemes of the devil. [12] For we do not wrestle against flesh and blood, but against the rulers, against the authorities, against the cosmic powers over this present darkness, against the spiritual forces of evil in the heavenly places. [13] Therefore take up the whole armor of God, that you may be able to withstand in the evil day, and having done all, to stand firm. [14] Stand therefore, having fastened on the belt of truth, and having put on the breastplate of righteousness, [15] and, as shoes for your feet, having put on the readiness given by

the gospel of peace. [16] In all circumstances take up the shield of faith, with which you can extinguish all the flaming darts of the evil one; [17] and take the helmet of salvation, and the sword of the Spirit, which is the word of God, [18] praying at all times in the Spirit, with all prayer and supplication. To that end, keep alert with all perseverance, making supplication for all the saints.

4. The Great Boston Fire was such a monstrosity that it was seen by those in ships as far away as the coast of Maine. The glow of the fire was immense, and during the dark of the night, it had sailors awestruck. In the same way, destructive fires within a church likewise command an audience.

    a. Who notices when a church is crippled or shut down by a satanic fire?

    b. What impact do these fires have on believers?

    c. What impact do they have on non-believers?

5. Many churches are in terrible predicaments, and their members sometimes feel like they're

holding on to pieces of a broken and dying church while they hope for a miracle.

   a. Whether or not your church is on the verge of total collapse, what would be your desire and prayer for churches that are facing this worst-case scenario?

   b. If your church seems to be far from the brink of closing its doors, how crucial do you believe it is to biblically fireproof your church *before* negativity wreaks havoc on your church?

6. A church must have a multitude of members willing to appropriately fight fires of negativity if it's going to be the church God intended for it to be. In fact, *entire* church families should be engaged within firefighting efforts, if possible.

   a. How willing are you to join with others in your church in preventing and extinguishing destructive fires within your church, and why?

   b. Why might some individuals within your church be apathetic toward firefighting efforts, and what (if anything) can be done to engage them in the battle?

<u>Before You Dismiss</u>:

Close the session with prayer. Ask God to help each member of your church to become engaged in biblically fighting fires of negativity within your church. If your church is on the cusp of total annihilation, thank God for being powerful enough to "give life to the dead and call into existence the things that do not exist" (Romans 4:17), when he's willing.

2

Fire Call Boxes Were Locked
Never Lock Up Your Ministry Potential

This session corresponds with Chapter Two,
which begins on page 11.

How to Begin:

Open the session with prayer. Ask God to allow the discussion to be encouraging and beneficial.

Ice-Breaker Questions:

1. What grabbed your attention the most in this chapter? In other words, what opened your eyes and led you to think about things you may not have thought about before?

2. Was there a biblical passage discussed in this chapter that really stepped on your toes?

<u>Other Questions</u>:

3. Paul and Barnabas often faced troubles on their
    missionary journeys. Read about their ministry
    in Iconium in Acts 14:1-7 (below).

    a. How did Paul and Barnabas immediately
       react to the trouble that was stirred up
       against them in Iconium? Did they flee
       or persist in their ministry (verse 3)?

    b. Why did Paul and Barnabas finally leave
       Iconium (verses 5-6)?

    c. When God led Paul and Barnabas to other
       regions, what did they do? Did they sit
       back in fear of experiencing yet another
       life-threatening situation, or did they
       continue ministering as they had done
       before (verse 7)?

    d. Why do you think Paul and Barnabas
       never became locked fire call boxes?

Acts 14:1-7
**¹ Now at Iconium they entered together
into the Jewish synagogue and spoke in
such a way that a great number of both
Jews and Greeks believed. ² But
the unbelieving Jews stirred up the
Gentiles and poisoned their minds
against the brothers. ³ So they remained
for a long time, speaking boldly for the
Lord, who bore witness to the word of his**

grace, granting signs and wonders to be done by their hands. [4] But the people of the city were divided; some sided with the Jews and some with the apostles. [5] When an attempt was made by both Gentiles and Jews, with their rulers, to mistreat them and to stone them, [6] they learned of it and fled to Lystra and Derbe, cities of Lycaonia, and to the surrounding country, [7] and there they continued to preach the gospel.

4. Despite the wishes of some, there are no "upstanding citizen" ministry opportunities wherein abuse *never* happens.

   a. Why do you think this is the case?

   b. Why does Satan like to convince people that a pain-free opportunity awaits them someplace down the road?

5. The chapter discussed having "a lizard's skin and a lamb's heart" when ministering.

   a. What does this mean, and how can Christ followers put this into effect?

   b. Which is harder to consistently achieve: a lizard's skin (the ability to withstand abuses) or a lamb's heart (the ability to minister with gentleness)?

6. There are a handful of ways that Christ followers can strive to prevent burnout when serving, and two of those ways are provided below. Read and discuss the importance of each.

   a. How willing are you to engage in these practices?

   b. How willing is your church (leadership and others) to approve of these practices, and how capable is your church to carry these out?

   c. Why might fulfilling these practices be difficult at times?

Delegate Responsibilities: Moses' father-in-law warned Moses that he'd surely burn out and cause problems for himself and those he served if he didn't delegate some of his responsibilities to others (Exodus 18:13-23). Moses took that advice and spared himself and others any number of fires. Likewise, the apostles serving in the early church chose to delegate responsibilities to others so that they could focus on that which God had specifically called them to do (Acts 6:1-6). As a result, the church grew and matured. When individuals wear too many hats (either by their own choosing or because they feel it is necessary), fires of negativity inevitably occur. Responsibilities should always be delegated and shared long before individuals get so overburdened that they crash.

Take Periods of Rest and Recuperation (Sabbaticals): Jesus often took private excursions away from everyone, sometimes including his disciples, when he needed time alone to rest and pray (Luke 5:16, Matthew 14:22-23). In fact, Jesus also advised his disciples to slow down and rest after they had grown exhausted ministering (Mark 6:31). Everyone needs to take appropriate time to recuperate and power-up spiritually when ministry is involved, otherwise burnout occurs and church fires will pop up. No one can expect to minister effectively for extended periods of time without down-time for personal health (physically and spiritually).

7. Read the Apostle Paul's teaching in 1 Thessalonians 5:12-14 (below).

   a. What are some attitudes and behaviors that should be fostered within your church, regarding the treatment of those who serve the Lord faithfully? Don't get hung up on the phrase "over you in the Lord," as the treatment of all laborers within your church should generally be somewhat similar to the treatment (regarding your attitude and appreciation of fellow laborers) of pastors, elders, teachers, etc.

 b. How should Christ followers respond to those who are idle (perhaps locked call boxes), fainthearted, and weak (perhaps those on the cusp of burnout)?

 c. If applicable, describe a time when a fellow Christ follower ministered to you in one of these ways, and explain the impact that it had on you and your service unto the Lord.

1 Thessalonians 5:12-14

[12] We ask you, brothers, to respect those who labor among you and are over you in the Lord and admonish you, [13] and to esteem them very highly in love because of their work. Be at peace among yourselves.[14] And we urge you, brothers, admonish the idle, encourage the fainthearted, help the weak, be patient with them all.

Before You Dismiss:

Close the session in prayer. Ask God to help each member of your church to become willing to serve, despite inevitable abuses. Also ask God to help your church to create and sustain healthy ministry opportunities while eliminating hazards that lead to ministerial burnout. Thank God for the blessings (rather than fires) that come to churches wherein everyone serves, shares responsibilities, and takes necessary breaks.

3

Gas Supply Lines Were Not Shut Off
Know When and How to Bless Others

This session corresponds with Chapter Three, which begins on page 23.

How to Begin:

Open the session with prayer. Ask God to allow the discussion to be encouraging and beneficial.

Ice-Breaker Questions:

1. What grabbed your attention the most in this chapter? In other words, what opened your eyes and led you to think about things you may not have thought about before?

2. Was there a biblical passage discussed in this chapter that really stepped on your toes?

Other Questions:

3. When it comes to blessing others and preventing or extinguishing fires of negativity, each of us must seek God's direction regarding the manner and timing of our actions.

   a. According to Proverbs 2:1-8 (below), what must we do to gain needed wisdom from God (verses 2-4), and how do we do this?

   b. How does God respond when we vigorously seek wisdom (verses 6-8)?

   c. How does God shield those who walk according to his wisdom?

Proverbs 2:1-8
¹ My son, if you receive my words
and treasure up my commandments
with you,
² making your ear attentive to wisdom
and inclining your heart to
understanding;
³ yes, if you call out for insight
and raise your voice for understanding,
⁴ if you seek it like silver
and search for it as for hidden treasures,
⁵ then you will understand the fear of
the Lord
and find the knowledge of God.
⁶ For the Lord gives wisdom;
from his mouth come knowledge and

understanding;
⁷ he stores up sound wisdom for the
  upright; he is a shield to those who walk
  in integrity,
⁸ guarding the paths of justice
  and watching over the way of his saints.

4. Sometimes it's easier and quicker to bypass the processes of wisdom-seeking and to rely on your own flawed instincts, especially when negativity looms or you feel threatened (as with story of the blind man in the burning house). Joshua unknowingly struck a deal with the Gibeonites (God's enemies) during combat missions because he did not first "ask counsel from the Lord (Joshua 9:14)." Feeling threatened, Jesus' disciples wrongfully tried to squelch the works of a man operating in the power of God because their own understanding of the situation was faulty and they did not first seek direction from Jesus (Mark 9:38-39).

    a. When have you set out to do something with the best of intentions in a fiery situation, only to learn later that you should have sought wisdom from God before acting?

    b. How necessary is it to seek God's direction during fiery moments, when our natural inclination is to trust our instincts?

133

5. The Holy Spirit will often try to pull us in a direction that is contrary to our own intuitions, understandings, and desires.

    a. When has this happened to you, and how did you respond?

    b. Does our capacity to trust God increase each time we follow his leading over our own sense of direction?

6. According to the first chapter of Nehemiah, Nehemiah did not immediately jump into action when he learned of the dreadfully negative circumstances that his homeland of Jerusalem was facing. Instead, he spent "days" (Nehemiah 1:4) fasting and praying before he set out to remedy the situation that had besieged his people. Ultimately, after much prayer, he was led to speak to his king and ask for permission and provisions to head back to his homeland for some firefighting. And yet, as Nehemiah was speaking with the king, what did he *continue* to do before going into detail about his requests? Read Nehemiah 2:1-8 (below), and pay attention to verse 4.

    a. How important is it that we continue to seek divine direction as we take the steps that God directs us to take?

b. What is the greatest benefit to those who continue seeking and trusting God's guidance (verse 8)?

Nehemiah 2:1-8

1 In the month of Nisan, in the twentieth year of King Artaxerxes, when wine was before him, I took up the wine and gave it to the king. Now I had not been sad in his presence. 2 And the king said to me, "Why is your face sad, seeing you are not sick? This is nothing but sadness of the heart." Then I was very much afraid. 3 I said to the king, "Let the king live forever! Why should not my face be sad, when the city, the place of my fathers' graves, lies in ruins, and its gates have been destroyed by fire?" 4 Then the king said to me, "What are you requesting?" So I prayed to the God of heaven. 5 And I said to the king, "If it pleases the king, and if your servant has found favor in your sight, that you send me to Judah, to the city of my fathers' graves, that I may rebuild it." 6 And the king said to me (the queen sitting beside him), "How long will you be gone, and when will you return?" So it pleased the king to send me when I had given him a time. 7 And I said to the king, "If it pleases the king, let letters be given me to the governors of the province Beyond the River, that they may let me pass through until I come to Judah, 8 and a letter to Asaph, the keeper of the king's forest, that

he may give me timber to make beams for the gates of the fortress of the temple, and for the wall of the city, and for the house that I shall occupy." And the king granted me what I asked, for the good hand of my God was upon me.

Before You Dismiss:

Close the session in prayer. Ask God to help each member of your church to cultivate a lifestyle in which wisdom-seeking occurs faithfully and often. Thank God for making straight paths (especially within fiery situations) for those who trust him with all of their hearts and lean not on their own understandings (Proverbs 3:5-6).

Water Power Was Insufficient
Rely on Fresh Power From God

This session corresponds with Chapter Four,
which begins on page 33.

<u>How to Begin</u>:

Open the session with prayer. Ask God to allow the discussion to be encouraging and beneficial.

<u>Ice-Breaker Questions</u>:

1. What grabbed your attention the most in this chapter? In other words, what opened your eyes and led you to think about things you may not have thought about before?

2. Was there a biblical passage discussed in this chapter that really stepped on your toes?

Other Questions:

3. This chapter discussed three reasons why church members (or attenders) often fail to walk in the power of God: (1) They do not have his power, as they do not belong to him. (2) They are more concerned with *talking* about power than *living* in power. (3) Their power is greatly weakened by lifestyles of sin that have not been eradicated.

    a. Which of these items do you believe is most prevalent in churches today?

    b. How important is it for the life of your church that all three of these items are always appropriately and consistently addressed?

4. According to Proverbs 14:23 (below), "mere talk" doesn't accomplish anything good.

    a. What must be done before good things occur?

    b. How can your church profit (or benefit) when its members work hard at pursuing God-ordained missions, including fighting church fires, rather than spending time talking about bygone eras or dreams regarding the future?

Proverbs 14:23
**²³ In all toil there is profit,
but mere talk tends only to poverty.**

5. When it comes to acquiring clean and useful pipes (living holy and powerful lives), the Apostle Paul provided a four-step process for Christ followers to follow. Each step is crucial, and each step must occur in the proper order. Read the four steps below, as well as the passages from Colossians 3:1-17 that are attributed to each step, and then discuss the questions provided.

    a. Why is it important that each step occur in order?

    b. Which may be the hardest step to implement?

    c. How do Christ followers go about "putting to death" what is earthly within them?

    d. Are you willing to move through these steps perpetually to best allow God's power to be maximized within your life?

Step One: Set your mind on acquiring clean pipes and honoring Christ with your life!

Colossians 3:1-4
¹ If then you have been raised with Christ,

seek the things that are above, where Christ is, seated at the right hand of God. [2] Set your minds on things that are above, not on things that are on earth. [3] For you have died, and your life is hidden with Christ in God. [4] When Christ who is your life appears, then you also will appear with him in glory.

Step Two: Get rid of your old, clogged pipes!

Colossians 3:5-11
[5] Put to death therefore what is earthly in you: sexual immorality, impurity, passion, evil desire, and covetousness, which is idolatry. [6] On account of these the wrath of God is coming. [7] In these you too once walked, when you were living in them. [8] But now you must put them all away: anger, wrath, malice, slander, and obscene talk from your mouth. [9] Do not lie to one another, seeing that you have put off the old self with its practices [10] and have put on the new self, which is being renewed in knowledge after the image of its creator. [11] Here there is not Greek and Jew, circumcised and uncircumcised, barbarian, Scythian, slave, free; but Christ is all, and in all.

Step Three: Implement new, clean pipes!

Colossians 3:12-16
[12] Put on then, as God's chosen ones, holy

and beloved, compassionate hearts, kindness, humility, meekness, and patience, [13] bearing with one another and, if one has a complaint against another, forgiving each other; as the Lord has forgiven you, so you also must forgive. [14] And above all these put on love, which binds everything together in perfect harmony. [15] And let the peace of Christ rule in your hearts, to which indeed you were called in one body. And be thankful. [16] Let the word of Christ dwell in you richly, teaching and admonishing one another in all wisdom, singing psalms and hymns and spiritual songs, with thankfulness in your hearts to God.

Step Four: Do all things (including firefighting) in the name of the Lord Jesus!

Colossians 3:17
[17] And whatever you do, in word or deed, do everything in the name of the Lord Jesus, giving thanks to God the Father through him.

6. Christ followers can be powerfully engaged in preventing and extinguishing fires of negativity within their churches when they belong to God, they are living in fresh power, and their lives are clean and God-honoring. God's power is mighty within these Christ followers.

a. What does it look like when Christ followers are fighting fires with power? In other words, how are fires within a church handled when members are full of God's might?

b. According to Ephesians 3:20-21 (below), who is glorified when Christ followers are living lives of power?

Ephesians 3:20-21
20 Now to him who is able to do far more abundantly than all that we ask or think, according to the power at work within us, 21 to him be glory in the church and in Christ Jesus throughout all generations, forever and ever. Amen.

Before You Dismiss:

Close the session in prayer.

- Pray for those in your church who may need to place trust in Jesus.

- Pray for others who may already belong to Jesus but aren't choosing to live in his power, as they are merely talking about power instead.

- Ask God to help each member of your church to strategically and perpetually eradicate sinful lifestyles that hinder them from doing all things unto the Lord Jesus, including powerfully fighting fires of negativity.

- Finally, thank God for allowing Christ followers to be "strong in the Lord and in the power of his might (Ephesians 6:10)", and thank him for the blessings that come to churches with members who are powerfully preventing and extinguishing fires.

5

Instructions from the Expert Were Not Heeded

Make God's Word Preeminent in All Situations

.

This session corresponds with Chapter Five,
which begins on page 45.

How to Begin:

Open the session with prayer. Ask God to allow the discussion to be encouraging and beneficial.

Ice-Breaker Questions:

1. What grabbed your attention the most in this chapter? In other words, what opened your eyes and led you to think about things you may not have thought about before?

2. Was there a biblical passage discussed in this chapter that really stepped on your toes?

Other Questions:

3. We all have found ourselves in figurative sewers because we failed to heed one or more instructions from God's Word.

    a. When have you found yourself in a figurative sewer?

    b. Afterward, did you endeavor to obey the authority of God's Word so that you wouldn't repeat your folly?

    c. How difficult has it been to keep that commitment?

4. The early church was "devoted" to God's Word (in the form of the apostle's teachings, since the written New Testament was not yet available to them), and church members got along with one another, served one another, and witnessed consistent numerical growth (Acts 2:42-47).

    a. If modern churches are devoted to God's Word and keep it preeminent in all things, might they experience similar results?

    b. How desirous is your church to experience similar results?

5. According to Acts 17:11 (below), the author of Acts (Luke) described a certain group of Jews in

Berea as being more noble (virtuous and reputable) than others because of how they responded to the teachings of Paul that referenced Old Testament history and prophecy.

> a. How did they "receive the word" from Paul's teachings?

> b. What did they do regarding their Old Testament scriptures, and how often did they do this?

> c. Would you consider yourself to be as noble as the Bereans?

Acts 17:11
[11] Now these Jews were more noble than those in Thessalonica; they received the word with all eagerness, examining the Scriptures daily to see if these things were so.

6. Sometimes things can usurp the authority of God's Word within the hearts and minds of those who do not strive to consistently keep God's Word preeminent at all times.

> a. According to Mark 7:1-13 & 2 Timothy 4:1-4 (below), identify two things that are commonly placed above the authority of God's Word.

b. How do these two things act as sparks and fuel unto nasty church fires?

Mark 7:1-13

[1] Now when the Pharisees gathered to him, with some of the scribes who had come from Jerusalem, [2] they saw that some of his disciples ate with hands that were defiled, that is, unwashed. [3] (For the Pharisees and all the Jews do not eat unless they wash their hands properly, holding to the tradition of the elders, [4] and when they come from the marketplace, they do not eat unless they wash. And there are many other traditions that they observe, such as the washing of cups and pots and copper vessels and dining couches.) [5] And the Pharisees and the scribes asked him, "Why do your disciples not walk according to the tradition of the elders, but eat with defiled hands?" [6] And he said to them, "Well did Isaiah prophesy of you hypocrites, as it is written,

"'This people honors me with their lips,
    but their heart is far from me;
[7] in vain do they worship me,
    teaching as doctrines the
    commandments of men.'

[8] You leave the commandment of God and hold to the tradition of men."

[9] And he said to them, "You have a fine way of rejecting the commandment of God in order to establish your tradition! [10] For Moses said, 'Honor your father and your mother'; and, 'Whoever reviles father or mother must surely die.' [11] But you say, 'If a man tells his father or his mother, "Whatever you would have gained from me is Corban"' (that is, given to God)— [12] then you no longer permit him to do anything for his father or mother, [13] thus making void the word of God by your tradition that you have handed down. And many such things you do."

2 Timothy 4:1-4

[1] I charge you in the presence of God and of Christ Jesus, who is to judge the living and the dead, and by his appearing and his kingdom: [2] preach the word; be ready in season and out of season; reprove, rebuke, and exhort, with complete patience and teaching. [3] For the time is coming when people will not endure sound teaching, but having itching ears they will accumulate for themselves teachers to suit their own passions, [4] and will turn away from listening to the truth and wander off into myths.

7. James spoke about the necessity of both knowing and following God's Word in James 1:23-25 (below).

    a. What does James say will be the result for those who do exactly what God's Word says to do?

    b. Do you desire this result to occur within your life and the life of your church?

James 1:23-25

[22] But be doers of the word, and not hearers only, deceiving yourselves. [23] For if anyone is a hearer of the word and not a doer, he is like a man who looks intently at his natural face in a mirror. [24] For he looks at himself and goes away and at once forgets what he was like. [25] But the one who looks into the perfect law, the law of liberty, and perseveres, being no hearer who forgets but a doer who acts, he will be blessed in his doing.

Before You Dismiss:

Close the session in prayer. Ask God to help each member of your church prevent and fight fires of negativity as each consistently strives to follow God's Word on all occasions. Thank God for the blessings that come to those who both know and do what his word prescribes.

Looting Was Rampant

Never Seek to Personally Benefit from Negativity

This session corresponds with Chapter Six, which begins on page 57.

How to Begin:

Open the session with prayer. Ask God to allow the discussion to be encouraging and beneficial.

Ice-Breaker Questions:

1. What grabbed your attention the most in this chapter? In other words, what opened your eyes and led you to think about things you may not have thought about before?

2. Was there a biblical passage discussed in this chapter that really stepped on your toes?

Other Questions:

3. Gossip is sometimes responsible for starting church fires, but regardless of how negative situations originate, it's often the very thing that makes church fires grow into monstrous and wide-sweeping destroyers. Therefore, Satan loves to generate gossip within a church whenever problems arise; it's the perfect fuel for the kind of calamity he desires to see happen.

    a. According to Proverbs 26:20-22 (below), what are several items to which gossip is compared?

    b. When those items (like gossipers) are removed from a fire, what is the result (verse 20)?

    c. Why are some individuals so willing to be on the receiving end of gossip (verse 22)?

    d. How can you go about ensuring that you won't be a gossip's taste-tester when a gossip is on the scene, or when one contacts you on the phone or by way of social media?

Proverbs 26:20-22
20 For lack of wood the fire goes out,
    and where there is no whisperer,
    quarreling ceases.
21 As charcoal to hot embers and wood to

fire, so is a quarrelsome man for kindling strife.
²² The words of a whisperer are like delicious morsels; they go down into the inner parts of the body.

4. The number of Christ followers who foolishly convince themselves that they can gossip under the radar and still manage to honor the Lord by serving him and his church would probably be staggering.

   a. According to James 1:26 (below), what one word best describes the actions of a pious gossiper?

   b. What are some ways gossips go about deceiving their hearts? In other words, what are some excuses that gossips make for themselves, regarding why they allow themselves to gossip?

James 1:26
²⁶ If anyone thinks he is religious and does not bridle his tongue but deceives his heart, this person's religion is worthless.

5. It's easy to be like Ham. Hams selfishly do what they believe will benefit them in the moment, and they respect no obligation to honor and protect others. It's much more difficult to be like

Ham's brothers, Shem and Japheph, who took it upon themselves to honor and protect others (their father and their families), even at their own expense (Genesis 9:23).

  a. Where are you in relation to Ham and his brothers? In other words, how willing are you to "walk backward" into negative situations to protect others and your church?

  b. How much better off would your church be if every member had a "walk backward" approach regarding every fiery situation that popped up within your church?

6. Unfortunately, there are some occasions wherein damaging and embarrassing information *must* be shared with others, and chapter six discusses the heart and manner in which this should be done.

  a. What are some hypothetical situations wherein this may be the case?

  b. Do church prayer chains qualify for must-share information?

  c. Can church prayer chains sometimes morph into gossip chains that fuel fires?

7. Ephesians 4:29 (below) provides the perfect mandate for all Christ followers, regarding how we should endeavor to talk both inside and outside of our churches.

    a. According to the verse, what should *not* come out of our mouths, what should our words *do*, and what should our words *give*?

    b. How can this verse be applied toward inclinations to talk about negative church situations?

Ephesians 4:29
[29] Let no corrupting talk come out of your mouths, but only such as is good for building up, as fits the occasion, that it may give grace to those who hear.

Before You Dismiss:

Close the session in prayer. Ask God to help each member of your church to practice a "walk backward" approach when dealing with church fires, big or small. Thank God for the blessings that come to churches wherein members are constantly speaking in ways that build one another up and offer grace.

Bystanders Were Everywhere
Do Something or Get Out of the Way

*This session corresponds with Chapter Seven,
which begins on page 69.*

<u>How to Begin</u>:

Open the session with prayer. Ask God to allow the discussion to be encouraging and beneficial.

<u>Ice-Breaker Questions</u>:

1. What grabbed your attention the most in this chapter? In other words, what opened your eyes and led you to think about things you may not have thought about before?

2. Was there a biblical passage discussed in this chapter that really stepped on your toes?

Other Questions:

3. When church members watch public fires of negativity rage within their church without their doing *anything* to aid firefighting efforts, their inaction can often make matters worse. And yet, it's incumbent upon all Christ followers to survey their actions and behave wisely, in a timely manner, when evil is advancing (Ephesians 5:15-16).

   a. How crucial is it that all church members are willing to help wherever needed when negative situations require all hands on deck?

   b. Does aid rendered by church members always have to be in ways those members are called and equipped (for the long-haul) to minister? Think about those who held up Moses' hands and those who manually transported fire engines throughout Boston; were they meant to do this *forever*, or were they simply alleviating a desperate need in the moment?

   c. What are some desperate needs your church is facing wherein church members could lend their aid, even if temporarily?

4. In Romans 12:10-13 (below), the Apostle Paul outlined several things that Christ followers should *always* be doing, not just on occasion.

    a. How might these things be beneficial to your church family when practiced among all church members during fires of negativity within your church?

    b. Can a church member truly love and honor others within his church while remaining on the sidelines as a spectator during church fires?

<u>Romans 12:10-13</u>
[10] Love one another with brotherly affection. Outdo one another in showing honor. [11] Do not be slothful in zeal, be fervent in spirit, serve the Lord. [12] Rejoice in hope, be patient in tribulation, be constant in prayer. [13] Contribute to the needs of the saints and seek to show hospitality.

5. Every church needs a wet blanket brigade, which is a group of people (ideally the entire church) willing to consistently bathe the church in prayer during fiery attacks from Satan, as well as at all other times. In Colossians 1:9-12 (below), the Apostle Paul provided a list of things for which he prayed, regarding the Colossian church, and the list showcases how

we might go about praying for our own churches today.

    a. How often did Paul pray for the Colossian church (verse 9)?

    b. What is the first thing Paul prayed would happen (verse 9)? How necessary is a prayer like this during church fires?

    c. How did Paul want those in the Colossian church to behave (verse 10)?

    d. What kind of power did Paul pray the Colossians would have (verse 11)?

    e. What is the last thing Paul prayed about (verse 12)?

Colossians 1:9-12

[9] And so, from the day we heard, we have not ceased to pray for you, asking that you may be filled with the knowledge of his will in all spiritual wisdom and understanding, [10] so as to walk in a manner worthy of the Lord, fully pleasing to him: bearing fruit in every good work and increasing in the knowledge of God; [11] being strengthened with all power, according to his glorious might, for all endurance and patience with joy; [12] giving thanks to the Father, who has qualified you to share in the inheritance of the saints in light.

6. At some point after initially praying for the Colossian church, Paul was led to minister to the Colossians by writing to them a letter (the book of Colossians). When we pray for our churches, God often leads us to do more than pray.

   a. How willing are you to pray for your church at all times, but all the more during church fires?

   b. How willing are you to immediately respond in obedience when God leads you to do something in addition to prayer?

   c. How much safer would your church be if all members were praying over your church and responding to God's instructions with absolute obedience?

Before You Dismiss:

Close the session in prayer. Ask God to help each member of your church to become willing to step up and act during church fires, to become active in your church's wet blanket brigade, and to obey instructions from the Lord. Thank him for the blessings that come to churches wherein members selflessly serve one another and pray for their church.

Fighting Fire with Fire Backfired

Deal with Bullies and Others Without
Adopting Bully Tactics

*This session corresponds with Chapter Eight,
which begins on page 81.*

How to Begin:

Open the session with prayer. Ask God to allow the
discussion to be encouraging and beneficial.

Ice-Breaker Questions:

1. What grabbed your attention the most in this
   chapter? In other words, what opened your eyes
   and led you to think about things you may not
   have thought about before?

2. Was there a biblical passage discussed in this
   chapter that really stepped on your toes?

Other Questions:

3. There is never an occasion wherein "fire-on-fire" combat is biblically permitted within our churches. According to Romans 12:17-19 (below), which was referenced within this chapter, each of us should strive to behave honorably and peaceably in all that we do.

> a. Why is this mandate often difficult to carry out?

> b. When Christ followers believe (or claim) that they don't care what others think of them, especially when it regards their own behaviors within a negative situation, is this appropriate (verse 17)?

> c. Does striving to live peaceably with others always mean that there will be peaceful interactions with others (verse 18)?

Romans 12:17-19
[17] Repay no one evil for evil, but give thought to do what is honorable in the sight of all. [18] If possible, so far as it depends on you, live peaceably with all.

4. As Christ followers, we must constantly be mindful of our reputations. It matters how we come across to others, both inside and outside of the church. When a fire of negativity is being

fought, we can't allow ourselves to forget about our high calling just because we're in the heat of the moment and things are difficult. Read Philippians 2:14-16 (below).

   a. When is it permitted to grumble (to have a bad temper about something or someone) or to engage in negative disputes (verse 14)?

   b. When we keep our composure and act appropriately under pressure, how do others view us (verse 15)?

   c. What is the one thing (as our guide and help) to which we must cling, when trying to fight fires without being justly charged for stirring the pot and making negative situations worse (verse 16)?

Philippians 2:14-16
14 Do all things without grumbling or disputing, 15 that you may be blameless and innocent, children of God without blemish in the midst of a crooked and twisted generation, among whom you shine as lights in the world, 16 holding fast to the word of life, so that in the day of Christ I may be proud that I did not run in vain or labor in vain.

5. When dealing with church fires, it's incumbent upon us to always act honorably and peaceably, but we're also sometimes required to take unpopular stands, make tough decisions, rebuke and correct others, and appropriately deal with church bullies — all of which can be uncomfortable (and even excruciating) at times.

   a. Why is it important that we do both, without dropping the ball in either respect?

   b. Did God ever promise that firefighting would be easy, even when done correctly?

6. Not everyone who starts or propels church fires is a church bully. We all fall short sometimes, and our sins often need to be appropriately addressed by fellow believers in Christ (Galatians 6:1). Those sins can usually be handled rather discreetly, as repentance, forgiveness, and restoration can occur without names or details needing to go public. However, church bullies present a different situation altogether. Their tactics are very wickedly premeditated and strategic, and they usually have an audience that is aware of what they're doing and saying, even if it's not apparent to some in their audience that their intentions are evil. Because of these things, bullies must be *publicly* rebuked, in as much as their primary

audience (whether it be a small group of people or an entire church family) dictates.

> a. According to 3 John 1:9-10 (below), what are the sinful outliers that place bullies in a league of their own? In other words, what makes a bully different than everyone else?
>
> b. How do you think Diotrephes came to wield such power (to the extent of throwing people out of the church)?
>
> c. If John (or anyone else) had never appropriately dealt with Diotrephes, what do you think would have ultimately happened, regarding Diotrephes and his church?

3 John 1:9-10

[9] I have written something to the church, but Diotrephes, who likes to put himself first, does not acknowledge our authority. [10] So if I come, I will bring up what he is doing, talking wicked nonsense against us. And not content with that, he refuses to welcome the brothers, and also stops those who want to and puts them out of the church.

7. When combating church bullies, Christ followers should always take the high road instead of mirroring church bullies and adopting their

tactics. Just as the Apostle John refused to deal with Diotrephes in a negative manner (3 John 1:9-10), we should likewise (1) publicly call out bullies by name, (2) list their offenses, and (3) perpetually stand up against them without entering the fray of negativity by way of reciprocating their behaviors.

- a. Why is it often very tempting to resort to negativity (fire-on-fire combat) when dealing with church bullies?

- b. Which of the three steps used by John toward Diotrephes is the most difficult to take?

- c. While it may be easier to allow church bullies to carry on with their antics without being contested, is this ever healthy for a church (especially in the long run)?

- d. How many demoralizing or ruinous church fires could the average church extinguish if its bullies were handled appropriately? This is a rhetorical question, of course, but allow it to trigger discussion in the final moments of this session.

Before You Dismiss:

Close the session in prayer. Ask God to help each member of your church to behave honorably and peaceably in all that is done, including when fighting fires and dealing with church bullies, when the temptation to use fire-on-fire combat is at its highest. Thank God for blessing Christ followers with self-control (2 Timothy 1:7) and providing a means to endure temptation (1 Corinthians 10:13).

History Doesn't Have to Repeat Itself
Selflessly Love One Another

This session corresponds with Chapter Nine,
which begins on page 93.

How to Begin:

Open the session with prayer. Ask God to allow the discussion to be encouraging and beneficial.

Ice-Breaker Questions:

1. What grabbed your attention the most in this chapter? In other words, what opened your eyes and led you to think about things you may not have thought about before?

2. Was there a biblical passage discussed in this chapter that really stepped on your toes?

Other Questions:

3. When it comes to living worthy of our calling as Christ followers, the Apostle Paul laid out some pointers in Ephesians 4:1-3 (below).

    a. How does Paul say we are to live as Christ followers (verse 2)?

    b. Which of these items can be achieved with an attitude of selfishness?

    c. What's the difference between simply bearing with one another and bearing with one another in *love*?

Ephesians 4:1-3
[1] I therefore, a prisoner for the Lord, urge you to walk in a manner worthy of the calling to which you have been called, [2]with all humility and gentleness, with patience, bearing with one another in love, [3] eager to maintain the unity of the Spirit in the bond of peace.

4. Church fires are often started and fueled when individuals fail to love one another appropriately. In fact, Paul explained that individuals can figuratively consume one another when supreme love for others is not occurring (Galatians 5:15). Paul painted the picture of what genuine,

selfless love looks like in 1 Corinthians 13:4-7 (below).

- a. Which of Paul's descriptions of love is your favorite, and why?

- b. Which of these items is perhaps the hardest for individuals to carry out, when it comes to selflessly loving others?

- c. How easy would it be for Satan to produce divisive fires within church bodies operating with *this* kind of love for one another?

1 Corinthians 13:4-7

[4] Love is patient and kind; love does not envy or boast; it is not arrogant[5] or rude. It does not insist on its own way; it is not irritable or resentful; [6] it does not rejoice at wrongdoing, but rejoices with the truth. [7] Love bears all things, believes all things, hopes all things, endures all things.

5. Reverend Beckley implored his church (and all Bostonians) to grow in love, compassion, and commitment toward one another. He warned his listeners that it was impossible to stand a fiery test otherwise!

a. How much so does Reverend Beckley's message ring true today? Is it applicable to your church?

b. How willing are you to prefer and promote your church family over your own personal desires and preferences?

c. When you suffer a setback or place yourself at a disadvantage as you selflessly serve others, how hard is it to respond as did the poor man in Reverend Clarke's story? – He said, "If it's God's will, it ought to be my pleasure! And it shall be!"

d. When individuals fight to protect and promote their own desires and preferences, with little or no concern for their church family at large, what are the consequences?

6. Now that you've completed the book, you're aware of a number of firefighting methods that you and your church can use to prevent and extinguish fires of negativity.

a. Which chapter(s) meant the most to you, and why?

b. How eager are you to go about fireproofing your church, now that you know how it's done?

c. How willing are you to keep each of these methods on your mind so that you won't forget them? Might you periodically look back to this book as a refresher?

7. Look at the list of firefighting methods summarized below, as taken from chapter nine of this book. Circle the items that you believe may be a struggle for you, and talk about those items with your group, if you're willing. In the least, be sure to share those items with an accountability partner who is willing to pray with you and encourage you to stay on task.

- Step up and start serving where your talents are best used, even when doing so makes you susceptible to underappreciation and abuse.

- Always seek God's guidance regarding the best time and manner to do things, including blessing others and fighting fires.

- Fight fires with an abundance of fresh power from God, as you know and belong to Christ, live righteously, and endeavor to be more about living in power than talking about power.

- Know and follow God's Word, and strive to make God's Word preeminent within your life and your church on all occasions.

- Never try to personally gain from a fire of negativity within your church, but always do whatever you can do to extinguish fires and minimize damage.

- Never sit by and watch a fire of negativity destroy your church, but lend your aid whenever possible, pray fervently for your church, and do whatever God specifically directs you to do to prevent and extinguish fires.

- Fight fires honorably and peaceably, and deal with bullies appropriately, while never employing bully tactics of your own.

- And finally, selflessly love and protect your church family, as unity and church health (being in full accord and of one mind) is always as the forefront.

Before You Dismiss:

Close the session in prayer. Ask God to help your church family come to increase its love, compassion, and commitment toward one another. Thank him for the tremendous blessings that come to churches whose members are selflessly serving and promoting one another, while fighting fires of negativity in all the right ways. Conclude the prayer by repeating the words of Paul's prayer in Romans 15:5-6 (below).

> **<u>Romans 15:5-6</u>**
> **May the God of endurance and encouragement grant you** (us) **to live in such harmony with one another, in accord with Christ Jesus, that together you** (we) **may with one voice glorify the God and Father of our Lord Jesus Christ.**

Made in USA - North Chelmsford, MA
1194065_9781793448156
11.13.2020 1445